**A GUIDE TO
EFFECTIVE GOVERNANCE
FOR INDEPENDENT
SCHOOL BOARDS**

TRUSTEE
HANDBOOK

EIGHTH EDITION

by Mary Hundley DeKuyper

NATIONAL
ASSOCIATION OF
INDEPENDENT
SCHOOLS

ISBN 1-893021-55-6

Printed in the United States of America

The National Association of Independent Schools represents approximately 1,200 independent private schools in the United States and other countries. All are accredited, non-discriminatory, nonprofit organizations governed by independent boards of trustees. NAIS's mission is to serve and strengthen member schools and associations by "articulating and promoting high standards of educational quality and ethical behavior by working to preserve their independence to serve the democratic society from which that independence derives and by advocating broad access for students in affirming the principles of equity and justice."

To find out more information, go to the NAIS website at *www.nais.org*. To receive a listing of NAIS books, call (800) 793-6701 or (301) 396-5911.

Editors: Nancy Raley, Karla Taylor
Book designer: Fletcher Design/Washington, DC

ACKNOWLEDGMENTS

I deeply appreciate the members of the National Association of Independent Schools team who contributed to this *Trustee Handbook*. I particularly want to thank NAIS President Patrick Bassett, who generously shared his expertise on what constitutes good governance, and Kathleen (Kiki) Johnson, former vice president for institutional leadership, who left her imprint on every chapter of the previous edition and thus continues to inform this edition. Another helpful segment of the NAIS team includes the heads and trustees of its member schools and the executive directors of its state and regional associations. Many of them offered valuable suggestions on how to make this handbook more useful to its readers, both in substance and style. I also wish to thank Karla Taylor and Nancy Raley, who edited the manuscript.

I am deeply indebted to all the many trustees and heads of school with whom I have had the pleasure to work over the years. Their wisdom, commitment to their schools' missions, desire to make a difference in the lives of their students, and support of their faculties and administrations have enriched and educated me.

Finally, I especially thank the remarkable women and men with whom I have served as a trustee of two independent schools. My experience on the board of The Bryn Mawr School in Maryland was among the most rewarding of all my service on nonprofit boards. I wish all board presidents and chairs had the opportunity to experience the same kind of dynamic and warm relationship that I enjoyed when working with Barbara Landis Chase (head of The Bryn Mawr School from 1980-1995 and current head of Phillips Academy - Andover). I am now fortunate to serve as a member of the board of Far Hills Country Day School in New Jersey, where the board is committed to governance innovation and excellence and holds the school's mission, students, and faculty in trust. Through her words and example, Far Hills' head, Jayne Geiger, continually inspires me and all trustees to be the best we can be. She expects no less from her students, faculty, administration, and herself.

— *Mary Hundley DeKuyper*

CONTENTS

Acknowledgments iii

Foreword...ix

Introduction 1

CHAPTER 1
PRINCIPLES OF GOOD PRACTICE

Keeping the Mission and Serving as Fiduciaries of the School 6

Fiscal Responsibilities: Stewardship of Resources.....................................11

The Critical Relationship between Board and Head 13

Board Development: Recruitment, Retention,
     Recognition, and Assessment of Trustees...15

Organizing the Effective Board and Adding Value to the School.................17

Conduct of Individual Trustees 18

I'm a New Trustee. Now What Do I Do?..20

Hot Topics for Board Discussion 21

Sample Materials...23

Resources..25

CHAPTER 2
KEEPING THE MISSION AND SERVING AS FIDUCIARY OF THE SCHOOL

Trustees as Keepers of the Mission 28

Trustees as Legal Fiduciaries...30

Corporate Laws, Internal Policies and Procedures, and
     Third-Party Contracts 31

Local, State, and Federal Laws and Regulations.......................................32

A School's Financial and Physical Resources..34

Risk Management 36

Case Studies...38

Sample Materials...40

Resources..45

CHAPTER 3
DEVELOPING AND REVIEWING POLICY

What Is Policy? 47
Reasons for Policy..48
Board and Staff Roles in Shaping Policy...49
Policy Development 49
Procedure for Forming Policy..51
Communicating Policies..52
Legal Concerns..53
Budgeting for Legal Counsel..53
A Note on Policies and Accreditation 54
Case Study 55
Sample Materials...56
Resources...59

CHAPTER 4
DEVELOPING A SHARED VISION AND PLANNING STRATEGICALLY

The Need to Plan 62
Who Should Be Involved in the Planning Process?.........................63
The Basic Planning Process...64
Strategic Indicators for Independent Schools 68
Definitions of Planning Terms 73
Case Study 75
Sample Materials...76
Resources...77

CHAPTER 5
ASSURING THE FINANCIAL STRENGTH OF THE SCHOOL

The Need to Raise Money...79
Perceived Barriers to Involvement in Fund Development................81
The Role of Trustees in Fund Development......................................82
Types of Fund Development Activities 84
A Final Note on Elementary Schools and Fund Raising 85
Case Study 87
Sample Materials...88
Resources...91

CHAPTER 6
DEVELOPING THE EFFECTIVE BOARD

The Importance of the Committee on Trustees 93
Bylaws and the Committee on Trustees..95
Primary Responsibilities of the Committee on Trustees 96
Additional Tasks of the Committee on Trustees...................................97
Trustee Diversity 106
Other Important Elements of an Effective Board..110
Final Thoughts on the Importance of the Committee on Trustees............111
Dimensions of an Effective Board..112
Case Studies...113
Sample Materials...115
Resources 125

CHAPTER 7
THE RELATIONSHIP BETWEEN THE BOARD AND THE HEAD

The Formal Relationship..128
Areas in Which Formal and Informal Relationships Overlap....................135
The Informal Relationship...140
Final Thoughts..141
Case Studies...142
Resources 144

CHAPTER 8
THE RELATIONSHIP BETWEEN THE BOARD CHAIR AND THE HEAD

Responsibilities of the Chair in Relation to the Board...............................145
Responsibilities of the Head in the Chair-Head Relationship 147
Joint Responsibilities 147
Comparing the Roles of the Board, the Board Chair, and
    the Chief Executive..148
Acknowledging the Impact of Leadership Change and Turnover..............148
The Importance of Communication 150
Disciplining Trustees: A Job for the Chair..151
Teamwork Metaphors for Head and Chair 151
The Chair as Official Nurturer of the Head..153
The Chair as Communicator of a Serious Message 154
Case Studies..155
Resources 157

CHAPTER 9

RELATING TO MAJOR CONSTITUENCIES OR STAKEHOLDERS

A Multiplicity of Relationships..159
Interacting with Administrators and Faculty...160
Interacting with Parents..162
Interacting with Former Students 164
Interacting with Current Students 165
Interacting with Funders and Friends...167
Interacting with Neighbors..168
Working with Educational Associations..168
Case Study 169
Resources 170

CHAPTER 10

ORGANIZING AN EFFECTIVE BOARD

How Nonprofit and For-Profit Boards Compare 171
Boards' Organizational Structures 173
Boards' Standing Committees 173
Committee and Task Force Assignments...176
Board Size 177
Board Meetings 177
Board Meeting Frequency and Length 180
Board Officers..181
Additional Committees Found on Boards 183
Case Study 186
Sample Materials...187
Resources 191

CHAPTER 11

PERFORMING THE ROLE OF TRUSTEES

Duties of Care, Loyalty, and Obedience...194
Conflicts of Interest...195
Other Standards of Conduct 196
Fundamental Questions...199
Case Study 200
Sample Materials...201
Resources 202

Appendix 1 — Additional Resources 203
Appendix 2 — Parliamentary Glossary 209
Index...215
About the Author 220

CHAPTER 9

FOREWORD

"**Y**OU ARE A TRUST HOLDER.**" Although these words appear at the end of this primer on trusteeship, they are embedded in the details and recommendations throughout. By commissioning Mary Hundley DeKuyper (a nationally recognized expert on nonprofit boards and an independent school trustee herself) to bring an earlier edition of *Trustee Handbook* into conformity with current best practices, we at NAIS are reinforcing our commitment to independent school leadership as one of our primary purposes.

"You are a trust holder." In leadership training at NAIS conferences and workshops, we echo these words frequently. Indeed, one of our messages is that independent schools have boards of *trustees*, not boards of *directors*. This is because holding a school, its mission, and its future "in trust" implies a very different role than "directing the operation," which is the job of someone else — the head of school. The legal obligations of trusteeship that this book explores (duties of care, loyalty, and obedience) set the context for the role of trustee. Complications of that role are many, of course, especially when trustees are also current parents. Knowing that the role of trustee is primarily future-focused and strategic, and learning how to keep it that way, helps parent-trustees remember that their job is not to manage their kids' school today. Rather, their job is to create the school from which their children's children will benefit tomorrow.

Staying strategic, then, becomes a chief challenge for the board and its leadership. In part, our role at NAIS is to use our publications, research, and website resources to share with school leaders the most current thinking and trends to frame discussion at the local school level. As we enter the 21st century, it is not surprising that the top six strategic issues NAIS research has identified are the following:

1. Recruiting, retaining, and competitively compensating high-quality faculty.
2. Financing the school.
3. Managing technology.
4. Developing the 21st-century curriculum.
5. Communicating to internal and external audiences.
6. Creating more diverse and inclusive communities.

An imposing list, for sure. It makes in shorthand form the major point of this book: Boards that spend their time myopically focused on the short-term crisis of the moment (a change in dress code, the drop-off pattern for pre-school, or the shortcomings of the new soccer coach) cannot see the need to plan for the long-term growth and prosperity of the enterprise.

It is true that trustees are recruited for what they can bring to the school: typically expertise, resources, and the Three *R*s of trusteeship—a willingness to assist in raising students, raising image, and raising money. But in return, trustees benefit richly from knowing they're making a difference in an enterprise so important to their family and community. I would add that, in the larger context, trustees add value to the entire universe of independent education by appreciating and defending its chief distinguishing feature: independence itself.

Independent schools are independent in governance and financing. Unlike any other type of school, we govern ourselves via a self-perpetuating board of trustees and finance ourselves by setting tuition and raising money. There are no directives, nor subsidies, from the central office (whether it be the public school district or the church). What is powerful about the model is that this independence leads to four freedoms, the combination of which is our greatest source of strength:

1. The freedom to define our own unique missions.
2. The freedom to accept (and keep) only those students whom the school's mission dictates we can serve well.
3. The freedom to define our quality in terms of teacher preparation and credentialing.
4. The freedom to teach the truth, as each school sees it.

One of the major responsibilities of an independent school board is to guard the school's independence. By fulfilling this responsibility, the work the school does locally — and the decisions it makes regarding mission, admissions policy, and funding — actually takes on, collectively, far greater import for the model of independent school education itself.

As I move among the extraordinary independent schools that belong to NAIS (more than 1,200 of them in the United States and beyond), I am frequently reminded of Peter Drucker's mantra: "Leaders do the right thing; managers do things right." It is increasingly clear that boards must be leaders who help our schools do the right thing. It is also clear that boards must respect the boundaries of their roles, encouraging but not directing the head and his or her administrative team and faculty to do things right. In the tumult that is the daily life of our schools and their leaders, there are many gusts of wind that can and do blow ships off course. The strong board of trustees is the sturdy mast that maintains stability and supports the sails that propel the ship of school forward. This new edition of *Trustee Handbook* will help all trust holders who read and abide by its directions to stay on course.

Patrick F. Bassett
President, NAIS
August 2003

INTRODUCTION

WELCOME TO THE CHALLENGING and rewarding world of independent school trusteeship. You have joined with thousands of men and women who care deeply about the highly diverse schools they serve: preschools, elementary schools, secondary schools, K-12 schools, boarding schools, day schools, single-sex schools, coeducational schools, religiously affiliated schools, secular schools, schools in the United States, American schools abroad, schools for children with special abilities, and schools for children with disabilities. The trustees who govern these schools have agreed to accept critical responsibilities as they work to further their schools' missions.

To be an effective trustee and add value to the work of the board and the school, you need to be informed about all aspects of your school and about trusteeship. Whether you are a new trustee or a more seasoned one, this newly revised handbook can be your companion as you examine your governance role.

THE HANDBOOK'S AUDIENCE

The *Trustee Handbook* is designed primarily for trustees and heads. However, it can be helpful to other school constituencies as well. Administrators and faculty, especially those who interact with trustees on committees or task forces, should find the book useful for understanding the different roles of board and staff and the charges for specific committees. Since parents and graduates often serve as trustees or as non-board committee members, the handbook can help them understand their special relationship to the school and to the board. Consultants to schools in the areas of governance, strategic planning, and searches will find the information contained here useful as well.

HOW TO USE THE HANDBOOK

With the exception of Chapter 1, all chapters follow the same format. They first provide subject matter content and then case studies, sample forms, and resources. The case studies conclude with questions designed to provoke trustees to discuss common problems and propose potential solutions. These cases, as well as the ones available on the NAIS website and personalized ones trustees can develop themselves, are useful for enlivening board orientations.

One caution on the sample forms: Because each school is unique, the forms should be viewed as guides, not as the only way or the last word.

A CHAPTER ESPECIALLY FOR ORIENTATION

Chapter 1 contains an overview of individual trustee and corporate board responsibilities based on the NAIS Principles of Good Practice for Boards of Trustees and Principles of Good Practice for Trustees. It is excellent for orienting new trustees and administrators. Chapters 9 and 11, especially when used together with Chapter 1, provide basic, essential information for all independent school trustees.

CHAPTERS FOR GENERAL BOARD AND COMMITTEE ROLES

Chapter 2 — keeping the mission and serving as fiduciaries for the school

Chapter 3 — developing and reviewing board policies

Chapter 7 — the relationship between the board and the head

Chapter 9 — relating to other major constituencies or stakeholders

Chapter 10 — organizing an effective board (including using task forces and key committees, such as the trustee, finance, audit, development, and executive committees)

CHAPTERS FOR SPECIFIC COMMITTEES OR TASK FORCES

Planning: Chapter 4 — developing a shared vision and planning strategically

Fund raising: Chapter 5 — assuring the financial strength of the school

Committee on trustees: Chapter 6 — developing the effective board

CHAPTERS FOR TRUSTEES WITH LIMITED TIME

Chapter 1 — NAIS's Principles of Good Practice for Boards of Trustees and Principles of Good Practice for Trustees

Chapter 2 — keeping the mission and serving as fiduciaries of the school

Chapter 3 — developing and reviewing board policies

Chapter 5 — assuring the financial strength of the school

Chapter 7 — building and maintaining the relationship between the board and the head

Chapter 9 — relating to other major constituencies or stakeholders

Chapter 11 — performing the role of trustees

Please make the *Trustee Handbook* your own. Use it when you have a specific question, when you are not sure you understand some part of your governance role, or when you want to find out if there may be different ways to approach a situation that appears confusing or elicits conflict. As a trustee, you will find you can be most effective when you continue to learn more about your school and your role as a board member. You, along with your fellow trustees, are on an exciting journey. Bon voyage!

CHAPTER 1

PRINCIPLES OF GOOD PRACTICE

A S AN INDEPENDENT SCHOOL TRUSTEE, you have been charged with carrying out very important duties. This does not mean you've been elevated to a special status; you have not been coronated to serve on the board. You, in partnership with the head, provide leadership and a framework within which the faculty members enact the institutional mission every day as they teach their students.

However, there must be a final authority for the school, and that is the board of trustees on which you serve. The board can act only as one body. No individual trustee, not even the chair, can act for the board, unless the board explicitly authorizes an individual to do so. The delegation of authority should be covered in the bylaws or recorded in the board minutes. The board, as a corporate body, and you, as an individual trustee, are legally responsible for the school — for all that it does and does not do. Each trustee is equally liable for every board decision, whether or not you are present when the decision is made. As a board member, your participation in board deliberations is a critical ingredient in the success of the board and thus of the school.

In the increasingly complicated world of independent schools, boards of trustees, who serve part-time without pay, have delegated to the head the responsibility for administering the school and designing and implementing the curriculum. This delegation is done within the school's mission and broad institutional policies and is subject to the oversight of the board. (More in-depth information on the board's legal or fiduciary duties can be found in Chapter 2. The responsibilities of individual trustees are outlined in Chapter 11.)

Over the years, the National Association of Independent Schools has developed a series of principles of good practice in various key areas of school operation — including principles for boards of trustees and for individual trustees. The principles define high standards and ethical behavior.

The following is an annotated version of NAIS's Principles of Good Practice for a board of trustees and for individuals serving on the board. The complete NAIS principles appear at the end of this chapter; the numbers in the following lists correspond with the numbers in the original principles.

KEEPING THE MISSION AND SERVING AS FIDUCIARIES OF THE SCHOOL
(More information on this topic appears in Chapters 2, 3, 4, 6, 9, and 11.)

PRINCIPLES FOR BOARDS

1. The board adopts a clear statement of the school's mission, vision, and strategic goals and establishes policies and plans consistent with this statement.

In creating and reviewing the mission, the board must understand and concentrate on the unique focus and expertise of the school. It must realize what the school is *not* as well as what it *is*. Too many mission statements are almost generic — they could apply to many schools. Boards that truly understand the role of their schools in the communities they serve draft mission statements that, by themselves and without amplification, clearly articulate the vital, inviolate characteristics of these schools. Good mission statements do not explain "how" or "why." They communicate "what" in clear, inspiring, and guiding words. Mission statements last over time, but regular reviews of the mission are important so that trustees understand and support it. In reviewing a mission statement, it is just as valuable an exercise to intentionally affirm the current wording as to change it.

All strategic planning should begin with the mission statement and end with checking the new plan against the statement. The development of a vision statement, or a statement of a preferred state, is often the next step in the planning process. It is very important to know the desired end state for the school when the strategic plan is accomplished, or even for the years beyond the time frame of the plan currently being developed. The plan's strategic goal and action plans stem directly from the mission statement and the steps needed to achieve the vision. School policies must also be in concert with the mission statement. In fact, the whole school should live out the stated mission because this is how a school earns and keeps its reputation as an institution with integrity.

As a trustee, you understand and support the mission, articulate it wherever you are, and use it as a guidepost for making board decisions. You assure that integrity is a hallmark of the school for which you are a fiduciary.

2. The board reviews and maintains appropriate bylaws that conform to legal requirements, including duties of loyalty, obedience, and care.

The board's internal rules are found within its charter, bylaws, and broad institutional policies and plans — all of which should be in concert with the mission. Bylaws should facilitate the work of the board, serve as a reference point for major procedures, and be concise. Bylaws should be reviewed by outside counsel when first drafted and whenever there are substantial changes. If a parliamentary authority is cited (usually *Robert's Rules of Order, Newly Revised*), board members should have a basic knowledge of parliamentary procedure so that full discussion is encouraged, the rights of the minority are protected, and the majority can come to a decision. The board should establish broad institutional policies from which the administration can develop operational policies and procedures. Bylaws and broad policies are the basic governance documents of the board. The board's internal rules must also conform to the legal or fiduciary duties of the board: loyalty (duty to put the interests of the school before individual interests); obedience (duty to be sure that the school complies with all applicable local, state, and federal laws and regulations and all accreditation standards); and care (the duty to make good decisions with reasonable care).

As a trustee, you understand the bylaws and your fiduciary duties and seek to be an effective participant in board deliberations, helping to keep board discussions at the policy level.

3. The board assures that the school and the board operate in compliance with applicable laws and regulations, minimizing exposure to legal action. The board creates a conflict-of-interest policy that is reviewed with, and signed by, individual trustees annually.

This principle expands the "duty of obedience" mentioned above. The board should establish policies that address actions necessary to reduce risks and should require the head to report periodically to the board on risk-management actions he or she has undertaken. The board should adopt a conflict-of-interest policy, and all trustees should identify their potential conflicts and sign the statement annually. Conflicts will include those inherent in the dual roles a board member may play as a parent of a child currently enrolled in the school and as a trustee.

Examples of other risk-management policies and procedures are up-to-date personnel policies; appropriate student-discipline procedures; crisis-management procedures; and sufficient insurance coverage, including directors-and-officers liability insurance that covers board members for actions that are not criminal or willfully negligent. For access to professional expertise in a number of areas, the board should engage outside legal counsel on retainer, to be available to advise the board when the need arises. Attorneys can be valuable trustees, but a trustee should not serve as the school's legal counsel. The board needs truly independent advice.

As a trustee, you disclose your conflicts of interest. You also make sure that the appropriate risk-management policies are in place and that you are vigilant in assessing potential risks.

6. The board recognizes that its primary work and focus are long-range and strategic.

The board does not get involved in handling the operations of the school, as this is why it employs the head, who in turn employs the faculty and administration. Specific responsibilities within the head's own domain include curriculum development, admission and discipline of students, and faculty promotions and individual salaries. Instead of focusing on school operations, the board spends its time on broad institutional issues that are strategic, not tactical, and that will affect the future of the school even more than the present.

As a trustee, you focus on those issues that assure that the school will thrive in the future.

7. The board undertakes formal strategic planning on a periodic basis, sets annual goals related to the plan, and conducts annual written evaluations for the school, the head of school, and the board itself.

As noted in Principle No. 1 above, the board periodically undertakes a strategic planning process that stems from the board-approved mission statement. This is done to assure that the vision of the school's desired future can be realized. The board, in collaboration with the head, develops action plans with annual goals. These goals and plans need to be measurable and should be the basis for evaluating the school and the strategic plan, the board's self-evaluation, and the head during performance reviews. By adopting its own yearly, measurable action plan and goals, the board can organize its work around those issues that are truly strategic in nature.

As a trustee, you enthusiastically promote a culture of evaluation and participate in all appropriate evaluations.

11. As leader of the school community, the board engages proactively with the head of school in cultivating and maintaining good relations with school constituents as well as the broader community and exhibits best practices relevant to equity and justice.

The board is a collection of individuals who reflect a number of the school's constituencies. As such, it should be active in promoting the school's mission, policies, and programs to the school community and beyond and keeping the relationships positive in ways that are appropriate for the board. It is particularly important that the board exhibit its commitment to equity and justice through its own composition, practices, and public advocacy. The board and head of school must be in complete alignment on and publicly accountable for their actions and words. That is what leaders do, day in and day out.

As a trustee, you work with your fellow board members and the head to make connections with the school community and beyond that further the school's mission, program, and policies. You assure that the board lives out a strong commitment to equity and justice in all that you do and say.

PRINCIPLES FOR TRUSTEES

1. A trustee actively supports and promotes the school's mission, vision, strategic goals, and policy positions.

Trustees not only determine the school's mission, vision, strategic goals, and policy positions, but they must also be able and willing to articulate the mission in formal and informal situations. The school community and the world beyond look to trustees as the people, along with the head, who understand and support the mission and care deeply about the school. Therefore, each trustee is expected to be a visible advocate for the mission of the school and for the board's policy decisions, whether or not such positions are popular with all constituencies.

As a trustee, you are enthusiastic about the school — its mission, faculty, students, and curriculum — knowing that such enthusiasm can be very contagious.

2. A trustee is knowledgeable about the school's mission and goals, including its commitment to equity and justice, and represents them appropriately and accurately within the community.

Trustees need to understand all aspects of the school. They need to be aware of all major issues, and when they are not sure of the facts, they should seek the answers from the appropriate source or sources. However, they need to be sure that the issue at hand truly is a board concern rather than one for the administration or faculty. A hallmark of an independent school should be its commitment to equality and justice. The board should assure that such a commitment is lived out not only within the school but also in how the board is composed and how it acts. Trustees should be visible supporters of this commitment within the school community and in the community beyond. When trustees are involved in mission discussions and in setting and monitoring institutional goals, they become effective advocates for the school.

As a trustee, you serve as an informed, active school advocate.

4. The board sets policy and focuses on long-range and strategic issues. An individual trustee does not become involved directly in specific management, personnel, or curricular issues.

Trustees are required to be responsible for the school as a whole. As part of this responsibility, they set broad, long-range, and strategic institutional policies within which the administration operates the school. The line between *institutional policies* and *operational policies and procedures* is not always as fixed or rigid as was thought in the past. Input on institution-wide policies may be sought from a number of constituencies, but the board has the ultimate authority for the approval of such policies. The head may also seek advice on operational policies and procedures from a number of constituencies, but she or he retains the authority for the final approval and subsequent implementation. Boards and heads need to establish a climate of trust that encourages candid conversations whenever a question of board policy vs. administrative policy and procedure arises. Trustees need to understand how staff, parent, and student grievances are resolved and how the curriculum is developed. Specific issues in any of these areas are the province of the administration and faculty, and if a trustee is contacted, he or she needs to refer the issue to the head.

As a trustee, you keep your eye on the big picture and enable the head to run the school.

FISCAL RESPONSIBILITIES: STEWARDSHIP OF RESOURCES
(More information on this topic appears in Chapters 2 and 5.)

PRINCIPLES FOR BOARDS

4. The board accepts accountability for both the financial stability and the financial future of the institution, engaging in strategic financial planning, assuming primary responsibility for the preservation of capital assets and endowments, overseeing operating budgets, and participating actively in fund raising.

The board is organized so that *all* trustees can be assured that the school's finances are well managed and secure at the present time and for the years ahead. The board requires periodic reports on the status of all school funds and physical assets as well as on actual vs. budgeted financial performance.

The board approves the annual budget based on operational needs, the strategic plan's priorities, and financial forecasts for the next three to five years. The board requires an annual independent audit, which trustees formally approve upon presentation by the external auditors and the audit committee. Especially in its role as the fiduciary for the school's future, the board also oversees institutional capital assets and the endowment. In addition to overseeing the school's fund development program, each trustee actively participates in giving and raising funds. (See No. 11 below.)

As a trustee, you understand the finances of the school, actively participate in board discussions, and ensure that the necessary financial policies are in place.

PRINCIPLES FOR TRUSTEES

11. A trustee contributes to the development program of the school, including strategic planning for development, financial support, and active involvement in annual and capital giving.

As part of ensuring the financial well-being of the school, trustees contribute monies to the annual fund and any capital campaign at a leadership level equal to their ability to give. There is an expectation that all board members will make a personal gift to both types of campaigns — and that trustees will demonstrate their support at the beginning of the campaign. A fundamental rule of fund raising is that you must make your own gift before asking anyone else. This is especially important for trustees.

Once trustees have committed to a personal contribution, they need to participate in raising funds from others. The most effective method of soliciting funds is the direct request, but many individuals find this difficult. If some trustees have problems asking for major gifts, the school should provide training for them or offer other fund-raising activities in which they can use their particular skills and connections. Many schools that hold a number of special events find that their constituents, including trustees, become tapped out. A school should seek to have balanced sources of funds based on the needs articulated in the strategic plan. These funds should include tuition, the annual fund, income from grants, endowment income, and special-event income. Trustees need to be sure that the school has a clear, long-term development plan that allows the school to thrive and further its mission.

As a trustee, you will give and get — cheerfully!

12. Each trustee, not just the treasurer and finance committee, has fiduciary responsibility to the school for sound financial management.

Every trustee is responsible for the financial well-being of the school and as such must have a basic knowledge of its fiscal status. Most boards have a finance committee; others may have a subcommittee or separate committee that oversees and reports on financial activities. This committee can neither make policy nor decide which institutional priorities should be funded. However, it can tell the board what funds are available and then turn funding decisions over to the total board, which then sets priorities. The board as a whole makes all major funding decisions, such as approving the yearly operating budget, setting tuition, adopting financial policies, and agreeing to undertake a capital campaign and setting its goal.

As a trustee, if you do not understand the finances of the school, you should seek to be educated on financial matters and actively participate in board financial discussions.

THE CRITICAL RELATIONSHIP BETWEEN BOARD AND HEAD
(More information on this topic can be found in Chapters 7, 8, and 11.)

PRINCIPLES FOR BOARDS

5. The board selects, supports, nurtures, evaluates, and sets appropriate compensation for the head of school.

The single most important act of a board is to select the head. This process should take careful thought, be given adequate time, and occur only after the school's leadership (board, administration, and faculty) reaches consensus on the school's mission and major strengths and concerns. However, once the head has been selected and arrives on campus, the hard work of building and maintaining this special relationship begins. The board needs to support the head in formal and informal ways — paying the head well, keeping the board focused on the big issues while allowing the head to administer the school, being available for advice when sought by the head, etc. Funds should be available to support the head's personal development. Trustees should also offer the head positive as well as negative feedback.

One of the major ways a board supports the head is to conduct a fair, written evaluation of the head's performance every year. This evaluation should be based on criteria predetermined by the board and the head; it can include personal goals if the head wishes to receive feedback on such goals. It is important that part of the orientation of a new head involve a discussion of the evaluation process and the basis for evaluation during that first year of headship.

Often a subset of the board (the executive committee or ad hoc task force) conducts the actual evaluation. Frequently, a school seeks the board's input by means of an instrument designed for this purpose. Sometimes others beyond the board participate. A smaller group can gather the information and develop the written report, which is then shared with the head by the subgroup, or often just with the chair and one other person. The head receives the opportunity to respond, and the report or a summary is shared orally with the total board in executive session. This is one time when the head is not present at a board meeting.

As a trustee, you are committed to keeping the board's relationship with the head a dynamic and positive one. This includes participating in the head's evaluation as appropriate and supporting the head's personal development to help him or her become even more effective.

PRINCIPLES FOR TRUSTEES

9. A trustee has the responsibility to support the school and its head and to demonstrate that support within the community.

Wherever trustees find themselves, they need to support the head and the school. If trustees have questions or concerns, they should ask the head or board chair directly. Once an issue has been resolved by the head (if it is an operational concern) or by the board (if it is a governance matter), trustees must support the outcome. It is not enough to keep silent about such a decision; a trustee needs to be an active supporter of the resolution. If this support is too difficult and the matter is one of great import or conscience, the trustee needs to leave the board without damaging the board, the head, and the school. To leave the board is an extraordinary action and should never be done without careful thought. But to stay and disagree over time is inevitably damaging.

As a trustee, you must ask questions about major issues and participate in appropriate decisions. You respect and fulfill your private, confidential duties as a trustee to question, to think out loud, and even to criticize if appropriate. But you also respect your public role as a trustee to serve as an advocate, defender, and, if necessary, conduit (but not supporter) of dissent.

10. Authority is vested in the board as a whole. A trustee who learns of an issue of importance to the school has the obligation to bring it to the head of school, or to the board chair, and must refrain from responding to the situation individually.

Trustees come to the board with a variety of experiences, including special relationships with the school, most often as a parent or graduate or both. A trustee must guard against generalizing from his or her personal situation to that of a much wider group. This is one of the most difficult aspects of being a school trustee. You need to be careful not to be drawn into a situation where you probably lack full knowledge and over which you have no authority.

As a trustee, you are polite to those who contact you with a concern but firm in adhering to your trustee role. You refer the person to the head of school or the board chair, whomever is most appropriate.

BOARD DEVELOPMENT
RECRUITMENT, RETENTION, RECOGNITION, AND ASSESSMENT OF TRUSTEES

(More on this topic can be found in Chapter 6.)

PRINCIPLES FOR BOARDS

9. Board composition reflects the strategic expertise, resources, and perspectives (past, present, future) needed to achieve the mission and strategic objectives of the school.

The committee on trustees involves the board and others in identifying potential trustees who meet established criteria. The criteria should include the needed strategic expertise, resources, and perspectives to enable the board to be truly effective. The committee needs to be sure that the qualifications and qualities of new trustees further the work of the board, the strategic plan, and the school's mission. Diversity in all of its manifestations should be encouraged and celebrated.

As a trustee, you are ever on the watch for potential trustees and bring them to the attention of the committee on trustees.

12. The board is committed to a program of professional development that includes annual new-trustee orientation, ongoing trustee education and evaluation, and board-leadership succession planning.

The board-development process begins with the annual assessment of the board. Usually, this is accomplished through written instruments that help the board measure both its collective effectiveness and that of individual trustees. The board can establish plans for its own education and training activities based on this evaluation. The committee on trustees, responsible for board development and nominating processes, can use the evaluation to facilitate the recruitment of trustees who will fill identified needs. The assessment can also be used to measure the board's success in accomplishing its operational goals for the year before and to establish new ones for the year ahead. If the board evaluates the performance of the head, it is only appropriate that the board also evaluate the performance of the chair and the board itself, including the actions it takes regarding annual professional development about independent school governance.

The committee on trustees, in partnership with the board chair and head and based in large measure on the board assessment, should plan a formal board orientation for new trustees each year. On an ongoing basis, it should also plan annual board education and training for all trustees, never forgetting to cover governance topics that would improve the board's performance or correct any bad habits into which the board has fallen. Most often, the head facilitates ongoing educational and training activities, whether about trends in education, fund-raising techniques, or potential legislation that could threaten the school's independence.

It is also vital that the committee plan ongoing programs of professional development for all trustees on the topic of governance, including the shared roles of board and administration.

A team consisting of the committee on trustees, the board chair, and the head should plan for board succession so that there is always a large pool of trustees capable of serving as officers and committee chairs. Potential leaders should be given special training and committee assignments that equip them for future positions.

As a trustee, you participate in the annual board self-evaluation with candor; seek opportunities for training and education within and beyond the school; and accept a leadership position, if offered.

ORGANIZING THE EFFECTIVE BOARD AND ADDING VALUE TO THE SCHOOL

(More information on this topic can be found in Chapter 10.)

PRINCIPLES FOR BOARDS

8. The board keeps full and accurate records of its meetings, committees, and policies and communicates its decisions widely, while keeping its deliberations confidential.

An effective board keeps its most important records of business (such as board and committee meeting minutes, budgets and financial reports, institutional policies, and bylaws) up-to-date and ensures that they are accurate, concise, and timely. Every trustee should have a board manual that contains these items plus job descriptions for trustees, officers, and committees and other documents that facilitate effective participation in the board's work. Board deliberations should remain confidential until it is appropriate to communicate them publicly. When decisions are ready to be communicated, then all board members should be visible supporters of such decisions.

As a trustee, you make sure that all minutes and reports are sent to you before each board meeting. You review them thoroughly and prepare to ask questions and discuss the issues presented at the meeting. You keep all deliberations in confidence until they become public; then you actively support them.

10. The board works to ensure all its members are actively involved in the work of the board and its committees.

It is the board, and only the board as a whole, that makes major policy decisions, but it accomplishes its work through committees and task forces. The board's organizational structure should be as lean as possible while still allowing the board to focus on its work. Committees and task forces can increase their own effectiveness by including nonboard members from the school and beyond with needed expertise not found on the board. An added benefit from this practice is the opportunity to include potential board members on committees and task forces so that they can be evaluated before being asked to join the board.

As a trustee, you are an active member of at least one committee or task force. You work to assure that the board focuses on its own agenda and is organized to do so.

CONDUCT OF INDIVIDUAL TRUSTEES

All of the topics featured in this chapter focus on the board of trustees with implications for individual trustees. Additionally, however, there are five explicit individual-trustee principles that need to be highlighted. (More information on this topic can be found in Chapters 9 and 11.)

PRINCIPLES FOR TRUSTEES

3. A trustee stays fully informed about current operations and issues by attending meetings regularly, coming to meetings well prepared, and participating fully in all matters.

Just as the board accomplishes its work through committees and task forces, committees and task forces accomplish their work through the efforts of their members. The board itself is only as good as the collective wisdom of the trustees. Thus, trustees need to be informed so they can participate actively and effectively. Materials need to be circulated before meetings in a timely manner. Trustees need to read and understand the material and come prepared to enter into the deliberations.

As a trustee, you must plan to attend every board meeting and do so unless there is a real emergency. You prepare in advance, participate fully in the discussions, and facilitate the board's ability to make decisions.

5. A trustee takes care to separate the interests of the school from the specific needs of a particular child or constituency.

Trustees who are also current parents are at greatest risk of becoming involved with the needs of an individual child or with a faculty member or administrator. Conflicts of interest for these trustees may concern their own child, their child's teacher, other children, or faculty members. Difficult issues could include the setting of tuition, specific curricular concerns, and disciplinary actions. Another conflict of interest could arise when alumni trustees believe that any change from the good old days is a traitorous act.

Of course, the vast majority of trustees reveal any potential or real conflicts and work for the good of the whole school — for today and the future.

As a trustee, you bring your experience with you to the board table, and you serve as a trustee for the whole school community.

6. A trustee accepts and supports board decisions. Once a decision has been made, the board speaks with one voice.

The board makes decisions after providing opportunities for input and discussion. Sometimes trustees find that they are in the minority on an issue. Even so, they are expected to support the decision outside the boardroom. Supporting decisions with which you do not agree is not easy, but such advocacy is critical for successful governance. If a board member believes that a major decision goes against her or his conscience, the trustee should resign from the board.

As a trustee, you speak up during board discussions but support the will of the majority within the board and publicly.

7. A trustee keeps all board deliberations confidential.

Board and committee discussions need to be kept in confidence so that trustees will feel free to speak with candor during meetings, factions will be minimized, and a climate of trust will prevail. Examples of items that might need to remain confidential include recommendations in their formative stages, sensitive personal issues, and business options. If you are in doubt about whether to share information with a non-trustee, do not share it until you have checked with the board chair or school head. Never discuss individual board members' views on a pending decision or even on one that has become public.

As a trustee, you speak with candor during board deliberations but keep such discussions, and the views of other trustees, in confidence.

8. A trustee guards against conflict of interest, whether personal or business related.

Trustees may have personal or business-related conflicts. This does not mean they should resign from the board. They must, however, identify their conflicts on the annual conflict-of-interest statement and share them with the board chair. Trustees should recuse, or excuse, themselves from any discussion on items involving their personal or business life and may not vote on such items. The minutes should identify the conflict and the fact that the trustees recused themselves from the deliberations and vote. Trustees *do* need to bring their expertise and life experience to the work of the board. However, they must not forget that their fiduciary duty is to care for the whole institution.

As a trustee, you disclose any conflicts of interest and do not participate in or vote on any actions from which you might receive personal benefit.

I'M A NEW TRUSTEE. NOW WHAT DO I DO?

New trustees are often advised not to speak up for the first year of board service and instead observe the board at work. This is a great waste of intelligence and experience. As a new trustee you should:

1. **Learn about nonprofit, and specifically independent school, trusteeship.** If you come from the corporate world, you should learn about the differences between for-profit and nonprofit governance. See Chapter 10.

2. **Learn about the school as a whole.** If you are a current parent, you will need to know about more than your child's experience there. If you are a graduate, you will need to be updated on the school as it is today.

3. **Learn how the board operates and about its underlying culture.** Ask for a mentor from among seasoned trustees, if you are not already provided with one.

4. **Listen carefully and ask questions such as:**
   - "Why?" (Never settle for answers like "We have always done it this way" or "We tried that in 1991 and it did not work.")
   - "How does this further the mission?" or "What does this do for the students?" (Asking these questions can make you one of the most valuable members of the board. You have about a year to ask "naive" questions because you "don't know the questions not to ask." After that, others will realize that you have been around long enough to really understand the issues.)

5. **Get involved quickly in the work of the board** and share your expertise generously.

6. **Contribute a financial gift to the school,** making the school one of your top charities.

HOT TOPICS FOR BOARD DISCUSSION

As an independent school trustee, you follow the Principles of Good Practice for school trustees and work to ensure that the board follows these principles as it fulfills its responsibilities and accomplishes its work of school governance. But exactly what are you discussing, planning for, and evaluating at the board table? What are the hot topics that concern many trustees? The following list is not meant to be definitive. Each school has unique concerns depending on its mission, size, location, etc. However, there are many issues that cut across all types of schools and communities.

- Local, state, and national legislation or regulations that threaten the independence of independent schools.
- Recruiting, retaining, and rewarding faculty.
- Faculty salaries and benefits.
- Faculty professional development.
- Financing the school.
- Tuition levels, including who can afford the school and the potential loss of middle-class families.
- Financial aid: In what grades should it be offered? Should it be full or partial? What percentage of the budget should it be? What is the role of merit scholarships and tuition remission?*
- Fund raising (particularly special events, where small amounts of money are raised through many hours of hard work by volunteers) vs. philanthropy (especially major and planned gifts, where larger amounts of money are raised without the expectation of anything concrete in return and accomplished with fewer volunteer hours).
- Public funding of private schools (through vehicles such as vouchers, Department of Agriculture school lunch subsidies, e-rate technology funding, block grants, etc.), where the dollar benefits should be evaluated against regulations and potential loss of independence.
- Managing technology, including covering its cost and maintaining electronic security.
- Diversity issues, including the ethnic, racial, gender, and economic diversity of the board, administration, faculty, and students.

---

* A NAIS study found that from the school year 1991-92 to 2001-2002, tuition rose 31 percent for independent day schools (to $14,785) and 29 percent for independent boarding schools (to $27,560). The share of students receiving financial aid remained the same (about 16 percent), but the average award was up 44 percent to $7,980. These numbers have been adjusted for inflation.

- Sexuality issues.
- Provision of non-academic services, especially for families and children under stress.
- Board fund-raising roles. For example, do you want only wealthy board members? Should you have a requirement that every board member give or get a certain amount, or that all must make the school their giving priority?
- Moving from a board made up mostly of parents or graduates to a board of a new design.
- Board organization: what committees/task forces to have, number of meetings, time of meetings, and board development opportunities.
- Governance issues: What is keeping the board from being more effective? What are the governance differences and similarities between for-profit corporations and nonprofit independent schools?
- Relationships with neighbors and government entities.
- Crisis plans for all kinds of emergencies, including for potential weapons of mass destruction and terrorist attacks.

SAMPLE MATERIALS

NAIS PRINCIPLES OF GOOD PRACTICE FOR BOARDS OF TRUSTEES*

The board is the guardian of the school's mission. It is the board's responsibility to ensure that the mission is relevant and vital to the community it serves and to monitor the success of the school in fulfilling its mission.

The following principles of good practice are set forth to provide a common perspective on the responsibilities of independent school boards. The board and the head work in partnership in fulfilling these principles.

1. The board adopts a clear statement of the school's mission, vision, and strategic goals and establishes policies and plans consistent with this statement.

2. The board reviews and maintains appropriate bylaws that conform to legal requirements, including duties of loyalty, obedience, and care.

3. The board assures that the school and the board operate in compliance with applicable laws and regulations, minimizing exposure to legal action. The board creates a conflict-of-interest policy that is reviewed with, and signed by, individual trustees annually.

4. The board accepts accountability for both the financial stability and the financial future of the institution, engaging in strategic financial planning, assuming primary responsibility for the preservation of capital assets and endowments, overseeing operating budgets, and participating actively in fund raising.

5. The board selects, supports, nurtures, evaluates, and sets appropriate compensation for the head of school.

6. The board recognizes that its primary work and focus are long-range and strategic.

7. The board undertakes formal strategic planning on a periodic basis, sets annual goals related to the plan, and conducts annual written evaluations for the school, the head of school, and the board itself.

8. The board keeps full and accurate records of its meetings, committees, and policies and communicates its decisions widely, while keeping its deliberations confidential.

9. Board composition reflects the strategic expertise, resources, and perspectives (past, present, future) needed to achieve the mission and strategic objectives of the school.

10. The board works to ensure all its members are actively involved in the work of the board and its committees.

11. As leader of the school community, the board engages proactively with the head of school in cultivating and maintaining good relations with school constituents as well as the broader community and exhibits best practices relevant to equity and justice.

12. The board is committed to a program of professional development that includes annual new-trustee orientation, ongoing trustee education and evaluation, and board-leadership succession planning.

S A M P L E   M A T E R I A L S

NAIS PRINCIPLES OF GOOD PRACTICE FOR INDEPENDENT SCHOOL TRUSTEES*

The following principles of good practice are set forth to provide a common perspective on the responsibilities of individual members of independent school boards.

1. A trustee actively supports and promotes the school's mission, vision, strategic goals, and policy positions.
2. A trustee is knowledgeable about the school's mission and goals, including its commitment to equity and justice, and represents them appropriately and accurately within the community.
3. A trustee stays fully informed about current operations and issues by attending meetings regularly, coming to meetings well prepared, and participating fully in all matters.
4. The board sets policy and focuses on long-range and strategic issues. An individual trustee does not become involved directly in specific management, personnel, or curricular issues.
5. A trustee takes care to separate the interests of the school from the specific needs of a particular child or constituency.
6. A trustee accepts and supports board decisions. Once a decision has been made, the board speaks with one voice.
7. A trustee keeps all board deliberations confidential.
8. A trustee guards against conflict of interest, whether personal or business related.
9. A trustee has the responsibility to support the school and its head and to demonstrate that support within the community.
10. Authority is vested in the board as a whole. A trustee who learns of an issue of importance to the school has the obligation to bring it to the head of school, or to the board chair, and must refrain from responding to the situation individually.
11. A trustee contributes to the development program of the school, including strategic planning for development, financial support, and active involvement in annual and capital giving.
12. Each trustee, not just the treasurer and finance committee, has fiduciary responsibility to the school for sound financial management.

---

* The two Principles of Good Practice were revised and adopted by the NAIS Board of Directors on March 24, 2003.

RESOURCES

Adringa, Robert C. *The Nonprofit Board Answer Book II: Beyond the Basics.* Washington, DC: BoardSource,* 2002.

Andringa, Robert C. and Ted W. Engstrom. *Nonprofit Board Answer Book: Practical Guidelines for Board Members and Chief Executives.* Washington, DC: BoardSource,* 2001.

*Formerly the National Center for Nonprofit Boards

National Association of Independent Schools website: *www.nais.org.* For trustee resources, click on Resources & Statistics, then NAIS Resources, and then Governance/Leadership; or click on Government Relations and then Advisories.

NAIS Principles of Good Practice: Equity and Justice. See Sample Materials at the end of Chapter 6.

Widmer, Candace and Susan Houchin. *The Art of Trusteeship: The Nonprofit Board Member's Guide to Effective Governance.* San Francisco, CA: Jossey-Bass, 2000.

· · · · · · · · · · · · · · · · · · ·

CHAPTER 2

KEEPING THE MISSION AND SERVING AS THE FIDUCIARY OF THE SCHOOL

A S A TRUSTEE, you are a trust holder for your school. You care deeply for and are committed to your school. You understand your school's character. You uphold your school as it is now while envisioning what it can be. You are there for your school, and yet not involved in its management. You make sure that the school's mission guides all that the school and the members of the board do.

As a trustee, you are also legally responsible for the school — as an individual trustee and as member of the board. You make sure that the finances are well managed and secure and that the school obeys all laws and regulations to which it is subject. You see to it that the school has established and regularly reviews policies and procedures to keep risk as low as possible, with appropriate checks and balances for all those who handle funds. Obviously, neither a board nor individual trustees can manage the day-to-day operations of a school; that is why it hires a professional educator to serve as the head, and she or he in turn hires the professionals who make up the administration, faculty, and other staff. It is through the board's keeping of the mission, setting of broad, institutional policies, and periodic assessment that it assures itself and all stakeholders that the school has in place everything necessary to protect any school's most precious possession — its integrity.

TRUSTEES AS KEEPERS OF THE MISSION

What kind of school is this?

To maintain a school's integrity, the school's mission should be the guidepost for all major decisions. The board of trustees is the body that delineates the mission, adopts the statement that describes the mission at the very beginning of the school, and reviews both the mission and mission statement periodically. Trustees hold the mission in trust; they are the keepers of the mission. This does not mean that the board sets or reviews the mission in isolation. The board should seek input from administrators, faculty, parents, alumni and alumnae, and students and then consider these constituent viewpoints during board deliberations. However, the final decision to affirm or change the current mission and mission statement rests with the board.

STATEMENT OF PHILOSOPHY OR OF CREED

What is a statement of philosophy?

Schools often have statements of philosophy or creed that serve as their overarching principles. Such a statement sets forth in detail a school's educational beliefs, practices, desires for the students, basic values underlying the school's program, and so on. It is usually of some length and most often is drafted by the faculty and senior administrators under the head's leadership. The statement is then discussed and adopted by the board of trustees, just as the board adopts the mission statement.

THE MISSION STATEMENT

What makes a good mission statement?

Because each school is unique, each school's mission statement should reflect its individuality. During the board's discussion of a mission statement, trustees need to ask themselves, does our statement:

- Express the school's reason for being?
- Set forth the school's uniqueness and areas of competence?
- Reflect the school's philosophy, including its core values and beliefs?
- Identify those whom the school serves?

- State the organization's primary strategic direction?
- Serve as the guide for major decisions while allowing for flexibility in their implementation?
- Set a standard for evaluation of programs and services?
- Stimulate energy and commitment?
- Read clearly and succinctly?

Few mission statements can fulfill all of the requirements set forth above and be succinct, although there are some excellent exceptions. Boards must balance what is most important for the school at a particular time with a desire for brevity. The shorter the statement, the easier it is for a school community to remember it and be inspired to action. However, if the words are so brief, vague, and generic that they could apply to any school, great confusion could result. Today many schools have three versions of their mission and philosophy or creed statements:

- A longer version, but not more than one page, for official publications.
- A concise three- to five- point statement for quick reference and for media sound bites.
- A school slogan or motto of two to six words describing what the school stands for.

IN THE BOARD ROOM

The first step any board should take after adopting a mission statement is to communicate the statement with a rationale that explains the board's actions. This holds true even when a board has intentionally affirmed the current statement. To be a living statement, it must inform all board decisions as well as all other decisions in the school community. It is interesting to note that having a living mission statement helps the board focus on governance issues — issues that are of broad institutional concern. You, as a trustee, can add great value to the board's work by asking questions such as the following:

> Now that we have a mission statement, what should we do?

- "Why are we discussing funding a third soccer field when our budgets are tight, we cut back on teacher salaries, and our mission stresses the centrality of academics and our commitment to an excellent faculty?"
- "Have you thought of the implications of holding a slave-auction fund raiser when our mission stresses our commitment to diversity in all of its forms?"

The school's mission lives daily in the life of the school — within and beyond its walls. When making both major and minor decisions, a school may be tempted to stray from its stated mission for reasons such as increasing enrollment or garnering more funds. But when this happens, a school may lose its reputation for integrity, a loss that can cripple a school in the long run. Trustees need to be ever vigilant in their role as keepers of the mission.*

IN THE SCHOOL AND BROADER COMMUNITY

Often, trustees are amazed to discover that they are perceived as experts on the school. They do need to be knowledgeable about its program, major strengths and concerns, and, above all, mission. However, it is not enough to understand and support the mission; they need to be articulate, enthusiastic advocates of it. Trustees need to be prepared to defend and further the mission in formal and informal settings, be it the parking lot, neighborhood party, or athletic event. If you are uncomfortable with this role, you need to ask yourself why. Do you have trouble supporting the mission? Or are you simply unaccustomed to speaking out? If the problem is the former, you should resign from the board; if it is the latter, get help developing skills that will assist you in speaking appropriately and effectively.

Advocating for the mission can lead trustees to speak out for the independence of their school from inappropriate governmental regulations, for their students and their special needs, for independent education, and more. Trustees can be effective advocates because they are not paid to do their work for the school, and — as committed volunteers, citizens, and voters — they bring credibility to their stated positions.

TRUSTEES AS LEGAL FIDUCIARIES

What do you mean, I'm legally responsible for the school?

The role of trustee as mission keeper is one of moral trusteeship. But just as moral trusteeship is a critical ingredient in maintaining a school's integrity, so is legal and financial trusteeship. Individually and collectively, board members are legally liable for their actions and those of the school. Trustees are the fiduciaries of the school they govern. The board is the sole corporate identity; it alone can take action, unless such authority has been expressly delegated by the board to an individual or group of people. Such delegation should be put in writing and appear in the bylaws or board

---

* For more on this topic, see the monograph "Mission Statements" by NAIS President Patrick F. Bassett. Details available in the Resources section of this chapter.

minutes. Individual trustees cannot commit the board or the school unless they have been given such authority by the board, and this prohibition includes the chair, committee heads, etc.

There are four major governance areas where the board must actively exercise oversight function. They are:

- corporate law, internal policies and procedures, and third-party contracts;
- local, state, and federal laws and regulations;
- a school's financial and physical resources; and
- risk management.

CORPORATE LAWS, INTERNAL POLICIES AND PROCEDURES, AND THIRD-PARTY CONTRACTS

All trustees should understand and abide by the school's articles of incorporation (or charter) and bylaws because these organizational documents serve as the internal rules for the school and the board in the following ways:

> Who cares what the bylaws say?

- A school's articles of incorporation/organizational charter are filed with the appropriate state authorities and usually set forth the school's purpose, its legal authority, and any limitations to its powers. Changes need to be filed with the state.
- Bylaws are the procedures by which trustees govern the school, and changes or amendments must be made in accordance with procedures stated in the bylaws. Typical items in bylaws include how decisions are made; how trustees and officers are selected and elected; how the board is organized; brief officer and committee role descriptions; the governance reporting structure, especially the relationship of the head to the board; and so on. Bylaws should be reviewed periodically, and if amendments are proposed, the school's outside legal counsel should review them. (Note: It is very important for a school to have independent legal counsel; see Chapter 3.)
- Internal institutional policies are set by the board to ensure that a school's operations are conducted appropriately. The administration then develops operational policies and procedures that implement broad policies and puts them into practice. Typical institutional policies are found in areas such as financial management; personnel practices; criteria for admission, financial aid, and tuition remission; safety and

risk management; protection of students; school discipline; fund-raising policies (such as conditions for receipt of gifts and policies for building endowment); and confidentiality of information. Each of these policies would in turn have operating policies or procedures.

Here are two examples of this idea in practice. It would be the responsibility of the board to adopt a broad policy stating that the school will protect students from harm. But it would be the responsibility of the administration, under the leadership of the head, to create specific policies and procedures regarding who can pick up a child at school. Similarly, the board sets policy on financial aid in terms of the total amount of budget allocated to aid, the range in the percentage of tuition and fees it can cover, and the criteria for awards (including whether they should be strictly need-based or partially merit-based). However, individual board members never make or review specific families' financial-aid decisions because that is an operational duty of the administration (and because no board members should be privy to confidential financial information about any of the school's individual families).

These institutional policies and the resulting procedures are binding, and courts of law use what is in a school's stated policies to make decisions on disputes. Do remember this: *A policy is not a policy unless it is written down.* It also does no good if a policy is not communicated to those it concerns. (See Chapter 3 for more about policies.)

- Contracts between the school and third parties are binding. Boards need to have a policy that explicitly delegates the authority to sign third-party contracts to a few individuals and then sets forth the circumstances under which the full board needs to be informed about a contract. Most such policies require that one of the signatories to a major contract be a trustee.

LOCAL, STATE, AND FEDERAL LAWS AND REGULATIONS

What's the government got to do with us?

Just as every state regulates corporations, nonprofits and educational institutions have statutes that apply to them. Each locality and state's law is unique, and so it is critical for the board to be assured that the school is obeying the applicable laws and regulations. Trustees can conduct this verification by reviewing reports from the head to the board and board committees; by retaining outside legal counsel, who should periodically review policies and procedures; and by hiring an insurance professional (who does not sell insurance) to review insurance coverage and risk-management policies and procedures. Independent auditors can be a critical source of information on internal controls and potential business risks. Some categories of statutes are:

- Nonprofit corporate law.
- Educational licensing and regulations.
- Charitable solicitation laws designed to protect the public from fraud and abuse.
- State tax exemption. Federal tax-exempt status does not automatically convert to the same status for a state; in fact, most states require a separate filing.
- Health and safety codes designed to protect students, staff, and the public.
- Charitable immunity statutes. The federal government [42USC145011 et seq.] and most states have laws that limit the liability of nonprofits from third-party suits alleging wrongful conduct. However, few such laws have been tested in the courts.

Schools that have an exemption from federal taxes under Section 501(c)(3) of the Internal Revenue Code are also called nonprofits. Exemption from federal taxes, however, does not exempt a school from filing an IRS Form 990 each year. Also, schools must pay income-withholding taxes, FICA, and any state withholding taxes for its employees.

Trustees also need to assure themselves that the school is acting within:

- **Anti-discrimination laws.** All civil rights laws apply to independent schools in their employment practices and admission to the school, including the Americans with Disabilities Act of 1990.
- **The Fair Labor Standards Act.** This is the federal wage-and-hour law, including minimum-wage guidelines and guidelines governing who is or is not exempt from the wage-and-hour law.
- **The Employment Retirement Income Security Act.** ERISA regulates pension and health benefits for employees. It does not require that such benefits be offered, but if they are, they must be administered fairly.
- **Intermediate sanctions provisions.** The IRS has increased its scrutiny of nonprofits' "highly compensated individuals," usually the head of school and perhaps other high-salary administrators. To avoid the threat of having draconian "intermediate sanctions" placed upon the school, a board must be scrupulous in documenting that head com-

pensation, in particular, is based on market comparisons (using NAIS head of school statistics, for example) and upon a positive evaluation.

A SCHOOL'S FINANCIAL AND PHYSICAL RESOURCES

Why can't I just leave the finances up to the finance committee?

Often, trustees are surprised to learn that they are equally responsible for the school's financial well-being and oversight of fiscal matters. Treasurers and committees in charge of finance, investments (if separate from finance), buildings and grounds (if separate from finance), and audits can facilitate the resource-oversight role of the board. However, the total board is liable when anything goes awry. It is critical, therefore, that financial reports be timely and understandable so all trustees can be fully informed. Such reports need to highlight variances to the operating budget so that board members can ask questions based on these variances. Boards do not "accept," "approve," or "adopt" financial reports because boards cannot be assured that the numbers are 100 percent accurate until they receive the annual audit from the external auditors. The board should not place itself in legal jeopardy by stating that they are accurate. But the yearly audited statements prepared by an independent auditor should be approved, since the auditor does testify to the accuracy of the audited figures.

The board undertakes its role of financial oversight through a number of actions and committees, which bring their recommendations and reports to the board for information or action. (See Chapter 10 for more in-depth information on committees.) Today, as boards move to fewer committees and more task forces, one committee — the resource committee — may oversee schools' resources. This committee is concerned with the traditional financial activities, as well as investments and buildings and grounds or physical assets. The following are functions that in a classic organization of the board are done by separate committees. The audit committee should always be an independent committee.

FUNCTIONS OF THE RESOURCE COMMITTEE

Financial oversight. The resource committee works with staff to prepare the annual operating and capital budgets and long-range financial plan; monitors all financial activity in greater detail than the board as a whole; develops financial policies; and brings all such items to the board for its approval, along with regular financial reports for the board's information. This committee works closely with the school's business manager or chief financial officer. Frequently, the treasurer serves as chair of this committee and is the board's point person with the staff on financial matters. Finance committee members must be careful to avoid taking upon themselves the setting of institutional priorities as they work through the budget.

Investment oversight. The resource committee monitors the investment of the school's endowment. Rather than manage the investments themselves, these committee members recommend an outside professional investment manager to the board for its approval. (Committee members generally do not have the time and/or expertise to manage school investments.) The committee interacts with the professional manager on a scheduled basis, recommends investment strategy along with other investment policies, ensures that income from gifts restricted to specific purposes is used solely for those purposes, and monitors investment performance against objectives established for the professional manager. (This can be a subcommittee of the larger resource committee.)

Physical assets oversight. The resource committee also oversees the well-being of all physical assets. With staff and appropriate outside consultants, it develops a long-range master plan for space-use for board approval and develops policies for board approval. Sometimes this function may take on added importance when a capital campaign is in the initial planning phase. The administration actually manages the buildings and grounds as part of the operations of the school. (This can be a subcommittee of the larger resource committee.)

FUNCTIONS OF THE AUDIT COMMITTEE

The audit committee consults with the independent auditor, recommends the annual independent audit to the board for approval, monitors the implementation of any recommendations on internal controls contained in the auditor's management letter, and can oversee risk-management activities, including major business risks.

FUNCTIONS OF THE DEVELOPMENT/ FUND-RAISING/ADVANCEMENT COMMITTEE

The development committee has general oversight of the fund-raising plans, both long range and annual. This committee, or a separate annual fund committee, implements the annual campaign, which should involve the board and other school constituencies. The committee may also be involved in planning and implementing special events, which often have separate committees constituted from the school community at large for each event. During the planning for a capital campaign, this committee recommends the goals and purposes of the campaign for board approval. Usually a school will establish a separate committee to implement the capital campaign, which is led by a trustee and involves trustees and other interested school supporters. The campaign begins with the solicitation of the board, then of major donors, and finally the whole school community through campaign activities and opportunities to give.

RISK MANAGEMENT

How could any member of this wonderful school community sue me? There is no way a board can establish sufficient policies and procedures to eliminate all risk and resulting lawsuits. But a school can manage risk to keep litigation to a minimum. The board's role is to ensure that the appropriate institutional and operational policies — such as personnel, student activities and behavior, crisis management, and financial management — are in place and that the school is following those policies and the resulting procedures every day in a consistent, fair manner. (See the Risk Management Checklist at the end of this chapter.)

A written conflict-of-interest policy, drafted by legal counsel, should set forth what constitutes a conflict. Then trustees and administrators should sign a form acknowledging that they understand the policy and identifying any potential conflicts they may have. It is interesting that a major conflict of interest for most schools occurs when parent-trustees vote on tuition. A few schools forbid current parent-trustees to vote on tuition, but this would be impossible for boards constituted entirely of such trustees. The chair should monitor any conflicts, and if a conflict should arise, the affected trustees should recuse themselves from any discussions or votes on the specific issue. Wherever appropriate, establishing a system for bids for major school purchases of goods and services is further protection against the appearance of conflicts of interest. Remember, even the appearance that trustees are enriching themselves, their families, or their businesses through service on the board — even if this is not the case — can damage a school's reputation.

One area that schools often overlook as part of risk management involves school publications. Every school wants to present the very best picture of its program, facilities, student body, and faculty. It does this through written material, videos, electronic media (including websites), and personal contact. In all of these interactions, the school and its trustees and agents must be accurate in their descriptions of current programs and practices and in their promises of what they can deliver. For example, imagine that School X promises that it offers a strong program in the arts but does not invest in building a program with well-trained faculty and dedicated facilities and materials. At the least, this discrepancy between promise and action can lead to a disappointed child and parents, who chose the school because of their interest in the arts. Today's independent school parents are products of the consumer age; they expect to see in action the program first described to them in the application process. Trustees should ensure that the school promotes itself in an ethical manner not only to avoid litigation but, above all, because it is the right thing to do.

Because of federal law and state statutes on charitable immunity, which protect nonprofit boards and directors or trustees from suits alleging corporate and individual wrong-doing, some legal counsels have advised schools that they do not need to have directors-and-officers liability insurance. However, other attorneys believe that schools should continue such coverage because few cases have been adjudicated. The D&O policies need to cover the fees of legal counsel as well as the monies awarded in a judgment against the school. Such policies do not cover criminal behavior or willful negligence. Therefore, the best protection against a suit is an active board of trustees that exercises its governance role with great care. (For ways in which individual trustees can protect themselves from potential suits, see Chapter 11.)

CASE STUDY

AN UNPLANNED DEFICIT

During a board meeting, the treasurer reports an unplanned deficit of $75,000 in this year's budget of $5 million. No audit is planned to confirm the deficit, and the chair claims that the deficit is "not a problem, because the finance committee is on top of the situation." No one at the meeting raises any questions or objections. Since this is your first board meeting as a new trustee, you reluctantly mention to the board that you received no copies of financial records during orientation. When you ask whether the shortfall results from a decrease in enrollment or an increase in expenses, the chair of the board tells you, "The finance committee is on top of the deficit, so you shouldn't worry about this."

What are the issues?
What should the head do?
What should the chair do?
As a new trustee, what should you do?

CASE STUDY

BOARDS OF A FEATHER

James Nelson enjoyed his service on the Academy board so much that he took on the chairmanship of the finance committee and devoted much time to furthering the Academy's impact and mission. He realized that a business associate, Michael Montagne, would be an asset to the board and managed to get him nominated and elected. Soon thereafter, with the board chair's endorsement, he selected Michael as a finance committee member.

In addition to having business dealings, James and Michael had known each other for years, lived a few blocks apart, and occasionally golfed on weekends. As Michael said, "We speak the same language." During a business lunch, Michael wondered aloud about the efficiency of Academy board meetings, saying, "Jim, you and I can do a mega-business deal in half the time one of those finance committee meetings takes, and those meetings are only dealing with a fraction of the funds we work with daily. There must be a way to streamline the meetings."

"Well, we get the agenda in advance, and we make up half of the committee," Jim replied. "I suggest that we talk about the agenda and then each of us will discuss it with one of the other two members to get their agreement. I see Martha at church, and your kids go to school with Paula's kids. I know that Martha would love to get back to her office sooner, and Paula often needs to leave finance committee meetings early. I suspect they would be grateful if we do the heavy lifting in advance."

At the next finance committee meetings, Paula, Martha, Michael, the Academy headmaster, and the business manager all listened as Jim ticked off approval motions of all the requests on the agenda without any discussion. The other trustees nodded their assent. The business manager looked pleased to be free of the questions she normally would have answered.

However, the head was troubled. He realized that these were busy, well-intentioned trustees who were pleased to finish a meeting in record time. But was this a wise way for them to make board decisions? Policy precluded their discussing board business outside of the meeting. On the other hand, why should high-minded reasons return them to a more time-consuming process? The head had a good working relationship with them, so was it even wise to interfere with their support? He wasn't sure, so he decided to speak to the board chair.

What should the board chair advise?

This case study is by Richard Barbieri. For more governance case studies, go to www.nais.org, *click on Resources and Statistics, on NAIS Resources, and then on Governance Case Studies.*

SAMPLE MATERIALS

RISK MANAGEMENT CHECKLIST

- ☐ Clear mission statement
- ☐ Crisis management plans
  - ☐ Adequate insurance
  - ☐ General liability
- ☐ Directors-and-officers liability

Written policies in the areas of:

- ☐ Blood-borne pathogens
- ☐ Conflicts of interest, with forms signed by trustees and administrators acknowledging the policy and identifying potential conflicts
- ☐ Personnel: hiring, evaluation, termination
- ☐ Staff evaluation and compensation (especially in regard to IRS intermediate sanctions provisions)
- ☐ Student code of conduct and discipline procedures
- ☐ Religious activity on campus
- ☐ Athletic safety
- ☐ Use of school bulletin boards
- ☐ Off-campus trips — including issues of adult supervision — locally, nationally, and internationally

- ☐ Utilization of buildings and grounds by the school community and outsiders
- ☐ Bids required for contracts for goods and services
- ☐ Financial management, especially checks and balances
- ☐ Investment management
- ☐ Admission
- ☐ Financial aid
- ☐ Gift acceptance
- ☐ A system to review policies periodically both internally and with outside professional assistance
- ☐ Up-to-date bylaws
- ☐ A strategic plan that has measurable action plans
- ☐ A rolling three-year financial plan
- ☐ Bonds for paid staff and volunteers who handle money
- ☐ Publications, videos, and electronic media that accurately portray the school, especially its admission policy, programs, and facilities

S A M P L E   M A T E R I A L S

INTERIM STATEMENT OF ACTIVITY

FOR THE MONTH OF APRIL AND
10 MONTHS ENDING APRIL 30, XXXX

	Month of April		10 Months Ending April 30, XXXX		(Over) Under	Year's Budget
	Budget	Actual	Budget	Actual		
INCOME:						
Tuition	$—	$—	$—	$—	$—	$—
Annual Fund						
Endowment Income						
Special Events						
Etc.						
TOTAL	$—	$—	$—	$—	$—	$—
EXPENSES:						
Salaries & Benefits	$—	$—	$—	$—	$—	$—
Instructional Supplies						
Faculty Development						
Trustee Development						
Maintenance						
Supplies						
Etc.						
TOTAL	$—	$—	$—	$—	$—	$—
Excess of Income over Expenses	$—	$—	$—	$—	$—	$—
Fund balance at beginning of the period	$—	$—	$—	$—	$—	$—
Fund balance at April 30, XXXX	$—	$—	$—	$—	$—	$—

Explanations of significant variances:

A.

B.

C.

NOTE: There was an operating deficit during the month of April. This could be a sign of problems, or it could be a usual occurrence during this month. The balance for the year is still positive.

SAMPLE MATERIALS

AUDIT COMMITTEE DUE DILIGENCE CHECKLIST

How to Use This Tool

This Due Diligence Checklist can be used in a variety of ways:

- The audit committee can complete the checklist annually and share the information with the board as part of its committee report.
- It can be part of the head of school's performance evaluation, if the head and board agree to this a year in advance of the actual evaluation.
- It can help monitor issue resolution.
- External auditors can modify it to include questions specific to your school and others suggested.

QUESTIONS TO ASK THE HEAD OF SCHOOL/ADMINISTRATION	YES	NO
1. Are we operating within our stated mission and philosophy?		
2. Are we providing the curriculum and services the school community expects?		
3. Is the board kept informed about all of the major issues facing the school?		
4. Have we identified the biggest business and financial risks we face as a school?		
5. Are we adequately managing those risks?		
6. Are regular financial reports issued to the board? (Do the reports contain a balance sheet and income/expense budget comparison?)		
7. Do we have a balanced budget (in which revenue is equal to or greater than expenditures)?		
8. Do we have adequate systems in place to monitor income, disbursements, and other financial transactions, including timely detection of errors and irregularities?		
9. Do we know if we are on track with the budget and/or the nature of significant changes?		
10. Are restricted gifts handled properly?		
11. Are we complying with the terms of grants and/or contracts?		
12. Are we complying with policies, laws, and regulations?		
13. Are all taxes and related forms remitted as required?		
14. Has any pending or threatened litigation been reviewed by outside counsel?		
15. Are we monitoring lobbying (real or perceived) activities?		
16. Are our information systems and data adequately safeguarded?		

S A M P L E   M A T E R I A L S

AUDIT COMMITTEE DUE DILIGENCE CHECKLIST

QUESTIONS TO ASK THE HEAD OF SCHOOL/ADMINISTRATION	YES	NO
17. Do we have a crisis plan or plans in place and communicated to the board and other appropriate individuals or groups within the school community?		
18. Have trustees, the head of school, and other major individuals in positions of authority signed conflict of interest statements, with potential conflicts identified and resolved?		
19. Are we carefully reviewing the performance of the school head and undertaking a formal evaluation annually?		
20. Is the school head's total compensation, along with total perquisites, monitored by the board, and does the chair review the head's expenses regularly?		
21. Are we pleased with the performance of our external auditor?		
22. Did we receive a management letter and an unqualified opinion from our external auditor?		
23. Have all the issues the external auditor identified been resolved?		
TOTAL NUMBER OF RESPONSES		

Prepared by: _____ Date _____

Reviewed by: _____ Date _____
              Chair, Audit Committee

SAMPLE MATERIALS

AUDIT COMMITTEE DUE DILIGENCE CHECKLIST

MEASURING YOUR DUE DILIGENCE SCORES:

MEASURE	OUTCOME
23 yes answers	Outstanding! Your major challenge is to keep up the good work and conduct continual orientations to keep the board informed, engaged, and active.
20-22 yes	Good work! Your school needs some fine-tuning, but is generally in good shape. *The audit committee, head of school, and chief financial officer (business manager) need to work on these issues.*
16-19 yes	Attention needed. There are some potentially serious issues that the board is not monitoring. *All of the entities listed above, plus the chair of the board, must make the issues a priority. Your external auditor, your state or regional associations, and NAIS can be of help here.*
12-15 yes	Warning! Major systems are nearing the point of failure. *All of the entities listed above, plus the chair of the board, must make the issues a priority. Your external auditor, your state or regional associations, and NAIS can be of help here.*
Less than 12 yes	Immediate action required! Key systems have failed. The administration and leadership competencies may be significantly impaired and unable to function. *You require outside consultation or intervention.*

This Due Diligence Checklist is based on the American Red Cross's advice to audit committees of its local chapters.

RESOURCES

Bassett, Patrick F. "Mission Statements" (monograph). Washington, DC: National Association of Independent Schools, 2002. Available at *www.nais.org*; click on Resources and Statistics, then NAIS Resources, then Governance and Leadership, and then scroll down.

Carver, John and Miriam Mayhew Carter. *The CEO Role Under Policy Governance.* San Francisco, CA: CarverGuide Series, Jossey-Bass, 1997.

Dalsimer, John Paul. *Understanding Nonprofit Financial Statements: A Primer for Board Members.* Washington, DC: BoardSource,* 1996.

*Formerly the National Center for Nonprofit Boards

"Doing the Right Thing: A Look at Ethics in the Nonprofit Sector" *Board Member — Special Edition.* Vol. 7, No. 5. May 1998: BoardSource.*

Lang, Andrew S., CPA. *Financial Responsibilities of Nonprofit Boards.* Washington, DC: BoardSource,* 2003.

Leifer, Jacqueline Covey and Michael B. Glomb. *The Legal Obligations of Nonprofit Boards: A Guidebook for Board Members.* Washington, DC: BoardSource,* 1997.

Zeitlin, Kim Arthur and Susan Zorn. *The Nonprofit Board's Guide to Bylaws: Creating a Framework for Effective Governance.* Washington, DC: BoardSource,* 1996.

CHAPTER 3

DEVELOPING AND REVIEWING POLICY

A S A TRUSTEE, you focus on broad institutional policies and leave operating policies and procedures to the school's head and administration. You make sure that board-generated policies further the school's mission and lessen risks to the school and its community through appropriate governance oversight and assessment. You are the ultimate custodian of the school's well-being, and you use your role in shaping, approving, and monitoring policies as a tool to achieve this end.

WHAT IS POLICY?

An institutional policy is a broad statement of purpose or limitation. It can be developed by the board, its committees, the head, or others within the school who perceive the need for such a policy. The board has the authority and responsibility to approve institutional policies; the administration implements these institutional policies through operational policies, procedures, and rules. However, if the policies concern governance issues, the board itself should implement the policy through governance procedures and rules.

What do you mean, "It's a policy"?

Example 1:

Policy: Because the school believes in the value of a diverse teaching staff, it will recruit faculty of color. (Approved by board.)

Procedure: The head of each division of the school will attend the statewide independent school employment fair for teachers of color. (Approved by head.)

Example 2:

Policy: Because the school believes in the value of a diverse board of trustees, the board will seek qualified people of color who believe in the value of an independent school education. (Approved by board.)

Procedure: The Committee on Trustees will ask board members to identify as potential board members at least one person of color whom they know personally from within the school or from the larger community. (Committee on Trustees develops the plan and implements it.)

As noted in Chapter 2, policies are not policies unless they are written down. They are not effective unless they and the resulting procedures are shared with the audience they are designed to affect — that is, the total school community, including faculty, administrators, students, parents, alumnae and alumni, funders, vendors, outside users of facilities, or any combination of these groups.

REASONS FOR POLICY

Why bother with policies? Don't they frustrate creativity?

Policies are designed to serve as tools for boards and administrations. Their purposes are to:

- focus energies and resources (in combination with the mission and strategic and operational plans);
- delegate authority while still allowing the board to keep control;
- provide a framework in which decisions can be made and work can be carried out;
- ensure consistency of actions, especially in difficult and stressful situations; and
- define the ways in which the school wishes to work and the board wishes to govern.

BOARD AND STAFF ROLES IN SHAPING POLICY

There is a widely held belief that the board sets policy and the staff implements policy. This statement is true, as far as it goes. Boards do set broad institutional policies, and staff then develops and implements procedures flowing out of the policies. However, administrators, under the leadership

> Isn't it confusing? Don't both boards and staff develop policies?

of the head, also develop and implement policies — broad operational policies. Although the head may ask trustees for advice on such operational policies, trustees should otherwise not be involved. Difficult problems arise when individual trustees interfere with the implementation of any policy, especially when students, parents, administrators, and faculty are involved. (See Chapter 9 for more information on the board's relationship with the school's many constituencies.)

POLICY DEVELOPMENT

Typical board-promulgated policies are:

> Which policies do boards typically set? Which do heads set?

- Mission statement
- Code of conduct/conflict of interest
- Bylaws
- Other governance policies/procedures (if not in bylaws):
  - Board giving
  - Board and committee meeting attendance
  - Board and committee participation, etc.
- Investment guidelines
- Annual budget
- Board self-evaluation

Typical policies and procedures promulgated by the board and head together are:
- Authorization, or delegation of authority, by board to head and by head to staff
- Crisis plans
- Financial procedures, especially checks and balances
- Admissions and enrollment (linked to mission and budget):
  - Numbers

- Type of students
- Admissions priorities (siblings, legacies, etc.)
- Employment terms:
  - Compensation philosophy, strategies, and goals
  - Salary ranges (the head decides on individual salaries)
  - Benefits
  - Course load for faculty
- Sexual harassment
- Safety and security of the school (people and property)
- Buildings and grounds:
  - Use by outside groups
  - Campus master plan
- Evaluation of the head by the board
- HIV/AIDS policy: staff, students, and educational efforts

Typical policies and procedures promulgated by the head and administration:
- Admission:
  - Application process, including decisions on admittance
  - Financial-aid process, including decisions on who gets what amount
- Administrative staffing:
  - Staff organizational table
  - Job descriptions
  - Evaluation
- Faculty:
  - Academic structure
  - Evaluation
- Students:
  - Code of conduct
  - Discipline procedures
  - Evaluation and grading system
- Program:
  - Curriculum development
  - Extracurricular, including sports
- Systems:
  - Administrative procedures
  - Information systems

No matter how carefully a board sets forth and seeks to understand the delineation of the board's role in policy development and approval, there will be occasions when confusion does occur. What trustees perceive as a board policy may be perceived by the head as an operational policy or procedure — and vice-versa. Usually, the solution to this disagreement is not to set more rules or guidelines, but to operate in a climate of trust and openness where differences of this type can be discussed and resolved. You, as a trustee, can play a critical role in this kind of situation by being a good listener, critical thinker, and consensus builder.

There may be times when a head will want the board's endorsement of an operational policy because the policy may be controversial — as with, for example, the HIV/AIDS policies developed in the late 1980s. Those policies were operational in nature, dealing with students, faculty, and staff as well as with curriculum content. However, HIV/AIDS was a high-profile issue within the school community and with the public at large. Once again, nothing is as simple as it seems!

For another way to think about relationships, see the "Design of the Partnership" diagram at the end of this chapter.

PROCEDURE FOR FORMING POLICY

The recognition of a need for a broad institutional policy can come from a number of sources: board committees, the chair, the head, the administration, and parents. However, the head is the one who most often confronts a situation that should have been covered by a policy and is not. She or he will bring to the chair's attention the need for a broad institutional policy to address the situation. Usually, the head will draft the policy in conjunction with the staff or with the appropriate board committee. The board will then adopt the draft policy upon the recommendation of the appropriate committee, which can be the executive committee when there are fewer standing committees.

Three leading thinkers on nonprofit governance, Barbara E. Taylor, Richard P. Chait, and Thomas P. Holland, have said that the board and administration need to work together on central issues that influence the effective fulfillment of the institution's mission. The question is not whether the issue is one of policy or of implementation; it is whether the issue is truly critical enough for all to work on it. Taylor, Chait, and Holland believe that few nonprofits can exclude the CEO (head) from policy development or the board from implementation. One of the examples they cited was a capital campaign, where the board must set policy and

> Who thought up this policy?

also implement it if the campaign is to succeed. Another example was a crisis of community confidence in which board members had to make decisions on crisis-related policy issues and then go out into the community to rebuild confidence by meeting with individuals, funders, corporations, and community groups. The authors believe that the old, clearly drawn lines between policy and implementation need to be blurred so that the issue, not an arbitrary rule, defines who is involved and how. (For the citation, see the Resources section at the end of this chapter.)

COMMUNICATING POLICIES

I never saw that policy. Where is it written down?

Remember, a policy is not a policy unless it is written down. Trustees need to see and understand the policies for which they are responsible. One problem is that board-generated policies are often scattered through years of board minutes and dispersed in various committee files and school offices. Although policies are in effect until they are officially repealed, many trustees are surprised to find that some policies are still technically in force, though not followed.

Imagine that 10 years ago, a policy stated in the board minutes that trustees need not attend meetings. Now they are expected to do so, but the policy was never repealed. Trustees, therefore, either need to have a notebook containing all board-generated policies, or they need a list of policies and where the full text is located in the school office. The latter presupposes that at least one up-to-date policy notebook actually is kept in the school's office. The board secretary should be responsible for ensuring that the policy notebook exists and is updated whenever the board adopts or repeals policies.

On the other hand, the handbooks for faculty/administration and for students should be shared with trustees for information purposes only. Board members do not get involved in the drafting of these handbooks.

Once you have navigated the turbulent waters of policy formulation, approval, and monitoring, you may wish to take a deep breath and then review a few of the policies your board has approved. Are they truly broad institutional policies? Who has played a role in shaping them? When were they set? What procedures have been developed to implement them? Then look at the list of board policies to see if any are missing. If no such list exists, suggest that such a list be developed for the board and that at least one policy manual be developed.

As a trustee, you are the keeper of the mission, and so you need to be sure that the policies work in concert with the mission. As a trustee, you are the fiduciary for the school, and so you need to be sure that there are policies in place to prevent wrongdoing. In fact, policies can further all aspects of your trusteeship role; they are major governance tools.

LEGAL CONCERNS

Years ago, many schools chose, often by default, to use as the school's lawyer any one of a series of attorneys who happened to be members of the board. This is not a procedure NAIS recommends. Inevitably, the attorney is faced with a major conflict of interest, particularly when it comes to resolving difficult cases in which the board itself may be the subject of litigation, real or threatened. And, alas, many frivolous lawsuits are taking the time — and dollars — of independent schools today.

> We need a lawyer. Can we use a board member?

Small schools with limited resources may still fall into this practice, but as a basic guideline, NAIS strongly urges schools to consider hiring an external lawyer on retainer. The attorney does not need to be an expert in school law. In fact, the generalist position can help, as most school law is public school law. Areas of legal expertise many independent schools have found useful include contract law, employment law, disabilities law, and sexual harassment law.

BUDGETING FOR LEGAL COUNSEL

One school we know has a special agreement with its counsel, which bills the school at a reduced percentage of the firm's normal rate (the difference is considered *pro bono*). The agreement is to accrue all bills incurred in one fiscal year for payment in the next. That way, if the school has an

> How can a school plan to budget and pay for such advice?

unusually high need to consult the attorney (something that can happen when unplanned situations, and corresponding unplanned expenses, emerge), the school can budget for the bills in the subsequent fiscal year. The result is that the head, board chair, and business officer never have to watch the meter, debating whether or not to call the lawyer.

Whenever you're in doubt, do call your lawyer. We only hope that your lawyer is not a member of your board.

A NOTE ON POLICIES AND ACCREDITATION

When your school prepares its self-study during the accreditation process, the governance-standards section will probably ask about the existence of policies in many of the areas noted above. This is yet another reason why it's wise to have an up-to-date policy manual.

CASE STUDY

SOCIAL PROMOTION AND BIG MONEY
BALANCING THE DEMANDS OF INDIVIDUAL TRUSTEES AND ACADEMIC STANDARDS

Smart Stuff Academy has a long-held commitment to educational excellence and promotes itself as a school for the academically serious. Johnny, the son of the school's most generous benefactors, is about to fail the third grade (again). His teachers indicate that Johnny is highly intelligent but chooses not to do his lessons. One senior board member takes up Johnny's cause, arguing that the board should require Johnny be passed on to fourth grade, both for social reasons and because his father has linked his next signif-icant dollar gift to his only son's progress through his alma mater. Several board members (and all of Johnny's teachers) balk at the pressure Johnny's father is exerting on the board. They claim that the school's academic standards would be forever compromised if the board caved in to his demand.

What are the issues?
What should the board do?
What should the head do?
What should the chair do?

SAMPLE MATERIALS

DESIGN OF THE PARTNERSHIP

Policies	Time and Attention Graph
Strategies mission survival leadership major	**Board's Decisions** Head's Advice
Partnership authorizations finance policies enrollment employment terms	**Shared Decisions: Board and Head**
Operational admissions staffing program systems	Board's Advice **Head's Decisions**

Above the diagonal line = allocation of board's time
Below the diagonal line = allocation of head's time

S A M P L E   M A T E R I A L S

MAJOR BOARD AND ADMINISTRATIVE POLICY CHECKLIST

Different schools adopt different written policies. Even so, the following lists serve as a useful point of departure for considering the types of policies your board and staff need.

Three efficiency hints: (1) When compiling board-meeting minutes, always print statements of board policy in **bold** or CAPITAL LETTERS to make them easily traceable. (2) Simplify the way you track board decisions by creating a cover sheet for each set of minutes with all actions noted and described. This cover sheet can also be kept in a separate file in the school office so that you only need to search one location to find out what was decided when. (3) Make sure that new-trustee orientations include either copies of the relevant minutes or a separate policy-statement document list, with dates when policies were passed, reaffirmed, etc.

Possible Broad Institutional Policies
(for which responsibility rests with the board of trustees)
Specific types of documents:
- [ ] a clear school mission statement
- [ ] up-to-date bylaws
- [ ] conflict-of-interest statements (forms that trustees and administrators sign annually to acknowledge the policies and identify real and potential conflicts)
- [ ] strategic plan with measurable action plans (as opposed to operational plans, which are usually the responsibility of the administration and faculty)
- [ ] rolling three-year financial plan
- [ ] crisis management plan

Policies covering:
- [ ] safety and security of the school community
- [ ] electronic security
- [ ] adequate insurance coverage (including general liability and directors and officers)
- [ ] personnel (including compensation and salary ranges)
- [ ] admissions (preferences, if any; desired school population to serve)
- [ ] financial aid (categories of eligibility; merit or need-based or both)
- [ ] financial management, especially checks and balances
- [ ] investment management, spending rate, etc.
- [ ] bonds for paid staff and volunteers who handle money
- [ ] bids required for contract goods and services
- [ ] gift acceptance and naming
- [ ] use of buildings and grounds by school community and outsiders
- [ ] publications, video, and electronic media that accurately portray the school, especially its admission policies and facilities
- [ ] systems to review policies periodically, both internally and externally, with outside professional assistance when needed

Continued

S A M P L E   M A T E R I A L S

MAJOR BOARD AND ADMINISTRATIVE POLICY CHECKLIST
(CONTINUED)

**Possible Important Administrative
Policies and Procedures**

(for which responsibility rests with the head)

☐ student code of conduct/discipline pro-
cedures/due process

☐ policies on admissions and dismissal of
students

☐ policies on hiring, evaluation, and termination of all staff

☐ a system for reviewing policies periodically, both internally and externally,
with outside professional assistance
when needed

☐ operational policies and procedures to
follow when implementing the strategic plan, with measurable outcomes

RESOURCES

Carver, John and Miriam Mayhew Carver. *Reinventing Your Board: A Step-by-Step Guide to Implementing Policy Governance.* San Francisco, CA: Jossey-Bass, 1997.

Chait, Richard P. *How to Help Your Board Govern More and Manage Less.* Washington, DC: BoardSource,* 2003.

*Formerly the National Center for Nonprofit Boards

Fletcher, Kathleen. *The Policy Sampler: A Resource for Nonprofit Boards.* Washington, DC: BoardSource,* 1999.

Taylor, Barbara E., Richard P. Chait, and Thomas P. Holland. "The New Work of the Nonprofit Board." *Harvard Business Review,* September-October 1996.

> **"The first responsibility of a leader is to define reality."**
> — Max Dupree

> **"We invite you to dream about the things that can really make a difference in the lives of students and faculty."**
> — Walter Burgin

CHAPTER 4

DEVELOPING A SHARED VISION AND PLANNING STRATEGICALLY

A S A TRUSTEE, you are the mission's trust holder; you serve as a legal fiduciary of the school's well-being; and you participate in the formation, approval, and monitoring of broad institutional policies. One of the tools you need to perform your governance role effectively is a strategic plan derived from the mission of and vision for the school. You may or may not participate directly in the planning process. But you will approve an amended mission statement or affirm the current one, and you may also approve a vision statement (though this is not a part of every planning process). You will also approve the strategic, institutional goals of the plan. In short, as a member of the board, you plan for the future of the school for which you care.

The strategic plan acts as a bridge between the school's mission and its policies. Such a plan will set forth what a school must accomplish in the next three to five years in order to thrive as it strives to fulfill its mission as effectively as possible. The plan takes into account the external and internal world in which a school exists; establishes goals and action plans that guide yearly operational plans; and sets forth methods and timetables for evaluation, which facilitates corrections to the plan as necessary. (See the section at the end of this chapter for definitions of planning terms. Though you do not need to agree with the definitions, it is important to understand how we use the terms in this chapter so that the process will make sense to you.)

THE NEED TO PLAN

> Should I spend valuable time on planning when there is so much else to do?

Trustees need to be convinced that strategic planning will be beneficial for the school as a whole and for the board in its governance role. The following are just some of the reasons to plan. A plan enables a school to:

1. Control its future. A school cannot control all the external forces with which it interacts, but it must not drift along, buffeted by whatever force or individual is strongest at the moment. With a strategic plan, the school can:
- consider options and choose the best path for the school at a given moment in its history;
- plan for contingencies;
- be more nimble and adaptable;
- have greater assurance that it will remain independent and true to its own mission.

2. Maximize resources. Resources, both human and financial, are tight for almost every school. Planning can help establish resource-allocation priorities to best meet the school's needs and fulfill its mission.

3. Develop and sustain a shared sense of direction. As the various school constituencies work together to assess the school's current status and planning for the future, they develop a shared sense of direction. This synergy can increase the probability of the plan's success.

4. Prepare for a capital campaign. Strategic planning should be the precursor of a capital campaign. Such a plan establishes the "why" that underlies the campaign case statement and allows the board to set priorities among a multitude of funding needs.

5. Inspire motivation for accomplishing the plan's activities. If the planning process includes all school constituencies, it can be a vehicle for motivating people to accomplish the established goals. Those involved in the planning process ultimately feel a sense of ownership of the plan and want it to succeed.

6. Instill quality or strengthen quality and accountability. A strategic plan can highlight the critical importance of quality in all that it does and establish ongoing procedures that evaluate the level of quality. The board can hold the head accountable for the fulfillment of, or progress toward, accomplishing the strategic plan's predetermined benchmarks. The board can assess its own performance by establishing an annual plan for the work the board does to support the strategic plan.

7. Improve public relations. A good process and the resulting plan can help a school's constituencies articulate where the school is going and why. Establishing clarity of mission and delineating measurable results allows everyone to tell the school's story internally and externally.

WHO SHOULD BE IN THE PLANNING PROCESS?

A critical component of any planning process is the constitution of the planning committee or task force. The quality, the breadth and depth of the plan, the ability to move the plan forward and generate enthusiasm throughout the school community — all these depend on who is involved in the process. A core group of seven to 12 from every part of the school community should facilitate the process. The board chair and the school head need to be actively involved. The board as a whole needs to be updated all during the process, as trustees must adopt the plan's institutional goals and major objectives and affirm or approve any changes to the current mission and vision statements. Faculty, administrators, parents, and alumnae and alumni also need to be involved. One individual can wear several hats, but no one person should represent a single constituency. Rather, everyone should bring his or her experiences to the planning deliberations and then plan for the school as a whole.

> Why can't a few trustees come up with a plan for the school?

Although it is not mandatory to hire an outside consultant to make the planning process effective, a consultant can be very helpful for keeping track of the process and encouraging all involved to participate equally. Consultant fees vary greatly and depend on the scope of work for which the school contracts. It is important to engage a consultant who does not come with a rigid, prepackaged process or preconceived outcomes.

Others in the school, beyond the core planning group, can be involved in the process during various stages, such as information gathering and brainstorming possibilities. The more inclusive the process, the wider the acceptance of the finished product — the plan. This inclusivity needs to be balanced with the importance of accomplishing the process in a timely and cost-effective manner.

THE BASIC PLANNING PROCESS

> **Where are we in the process — step seven or step 23?**

A planning process can have a multitude of steps and be very complicated. However, a simple process is easier to manage and explain. The following are the seven most basic planning stages.

1. Planning to plan.

- Get the board and administration to support the need for a strategic plan and recognize the plan's benefits to the school.
- Select the planning committee or task force and its leadership.
- Decide whether it's necessary to hire an outside consultant, and, if so, select and hire one.
- Establish the planning process and its timelines.

2. Gathering information about and assessing the environment.

If the planning committee or task force is not careful, this step can be time-consuming and costly. Because planners can never know everything about everything, they must set priorities about which information is most critical and how the committee should collect the needed information to develop the best plan. It's helpful to think in terms of two basic kinds of information gathering:

External information gathering is designed to answer the questions, What are the opportunities and threats in the school's environment? What's going on out there?

Examples of methods:

- Conduct surveys, interviews, and focus groups with various external groups about the major issues facing the community, public and independent institutions, and higher education.
- Do the same with internal groups about their perceptions of the external world.
- Collect census data for demographics.
- Collect data from NAIS and state and regional associations. (The NAIS website offers national trend data and customized benchmarks at *www.nais.org/resources/statsonline/*.)

Internal information gathering asks the questions, What are the school's strengths and weaknesses? How are we doing?

Examples of methods:

- Conduct surveys, interviews, and focus groups of both internal constituents and outsiders about their perceptions of the school. These people could include
  - Students
  - Parents
  - Faculty
  - Administrators
  - Alumnae and alumni
  - Administrators, teachers, and others from colleges your students go on to attend
  - Families who apply, including those whose children are admitted and those who choose not to attend
  - Funders
  - Community leaders
- If it exists, review progress toward the previous strategic plan.
- Collect information on internal trends, such as enrollment, tuition, fund raising, and financial aid.
- Collect comparison data about other schools you use as benchmarks and gather information from state and regional associations. (Again, contact NAIS for more information, including a constituent survey that is benchmarked against other independent schools.)

3. Developing the strategic plan's mission, vision, and goals.

Planning committees or task forces usually begin with a retreat of at least a day. The committee can invite other members of the school's many constituencies for the retreat, but the number should not grow beyond 20 to 25. Planning retreats can:

- Establish the school's mission and the statement that describes the mission or, if the mission and its statement already exist, examine them critically. It is just as valid to affirm the mission and its statement intentionally as to alter them.
- Develop a vision of the school at least 10 years in the future and a statement that vividly describes that vision. This can be done by developing a variety of scenarios that can be brought together to form the collective vision. (Not all planning processes involve this step, but establishing and communicating a vision, or a preferred future state, can energize and unify the school.)
- Generate strategic issues and set priorities based on an environmental scan and an assessment of the issues by the administration, the outside consultant, or both.
- Develop draft strategic goals that address the major critical issues. (The tendency is to establish too many goals. The fewer the better — say, five to seven.) Check the goals to affirm that they further the mission and will lead to attaining the vision.
- Draft the written strategic plan, which should include
  - a description of the planning process;
  - vision statement (if part of the process);
  - mission statement;
  - broad institutional goals, with accompanying rationales and underlying strategic priorities; and
  - explanation of next steps.

Note: Never forget that the mission is the key component of the planning process and its successful implementation.

4. Developing action plans and more detailed yearly operational plans.

These set forth how the school will meet each goal. Notice that action plans can consist of objectives and strategies or lists of activities. The staff, under the leadership of the head, shoulders most of the responsibility for developing and implementing such plans. Boards and their committees may establish their own yearly operational plans to focus the board on its own work to further the strategic plan.

- Establish responsibilities and the resulting accountability of individuals,

committees, task forces, academic and administrative departments, etc.
- Set timelines, remembering that you have more than one year to accomplish the plan.
- Monitor and evaluate the plan's progress at pre-established intervals.

5. Generate buy-in with scenario testing.

Share various scenarios about where the plans could lead with key constituencies to test the waters and see what excites people. By presenting the plans as a draft, you'll be able to vet them with small groups within the community even as you communicate about them more widely. The outcome should be greater buy-in. (Scenario-testing can also be a vital stage in capital campaign consciousness-raising and involvement of potential donors.)

6. Approving the plan.

Because the board of trustees is ultimately responsible for accomplishing the plan, the board officially approves the plan. Note that although the board approves the mission and vision statements and the organizational strategic goals, the board does not vote on operational plans unless they involve the work of the board or there are major costs involved in implementing them. In some planning processes, the action steps are developed only after the board has approved the goals. In any case, the trustees should not learn about the plan's content for the first time at the meeting at which they are supposed to approve it.
- Every trustee should be informed of the planning process all during the plan's development.
- Board committees can be included in the planning process where appropriate, such as assisting in information-gathering and brainstorming critical issues within the committee's area of responsibility. This can save the planning committee time and also build support for the plan among trustees who are not on the actual planning committee.
- The plan must be sent out well before the meeting where the board will be asked to approve it. At the beginning of the planning process, organizers must schedule sufficient time for the board to deliberate either at a board meeting dedicated solely to the plan or at a retreat for that same purpose.

7. Celebrating and communicating the plan (mission, vision, and goals) to all school constituencies.

- Use newsletters, meetings, or a special mailing (1) to outline the planning process and who was involved and (2) to set forth the mission, vision, and goals, along with their rationales.
- As the plan unfolds, communicate accomplishments at meetings of the board, staff, faculty, parents, students, graduates, and others. This will keep the plan alive and off the shelf!

8. Implementing the plan.

This is the most difficult, and the most important, part of the planning process. Will Rogers was right when he said, "Even if you're on the right track, you'll get run over if you just sit there."

Another variation on this process appears in a monograph on the NAIS website. Go to *www.nais.org*, click on Resources and Statistics, NAIS Resources, and Governance/Leadership; then scroll down to "Strategic Planning: The Eight-Step Model."

FINALLY, EVALUATE THE TOTAL PLAN AT LEAST ONCE A YEAR

What have we done?

Because evaluation is a board responsibility, initially the process should include all those involved in the plan's development. The board needs to assess the status of each goal and its strategic issues and make corrections when necessary. No one should ever believe the plan is cast in concrete. Circumstances change, and so should the plan where appropriate. Note that individual components of the plan may require more frequent monitoring by board committees or the total board, so the original plan's schedule should allow for these evaluations. Some boards use key indicators of success, where certain activities or goals that are critical to accomplishing the plan are highlighted at predetermined intervals. An example of another method of measuring strategic indicators follows.

STRATEGIC INDICATORS FOR INDEPENDENT SCHOOLS

Strategic planning and equally strategic execution are the hallmarks of a well-run business or school. In an era when independent schools are seeing their governing boards include many people for whom nonprofit trusteeship is a new experience — indeed, for whom independent schools themselves are a new experience — it is all too easy for some boards to focus on issues on the near horizon and become overly involved with the current school year.

The real job of trusteeship is to plan for and assure the school of tomorrow. That important task involves taking some regular measures of where the school has been, where it is today, and where it wants and is able to go next. Good trusteeship is like driving a car. Good drivers:

- Glance for a few seconds in the rearview mirror to be sure that there are no signs of trouble behind them — no bright, blinking lights and no sirens.
- Look down for a few seconds at the dashboard indicators of a school's speed and direction to be sure that there is sufficient gas and oil, their speed is appropriate, etc. This way, they know that the underlying systems are OK.
- Look ahead down the road, with their eyes on the horizon, to see where they need to go, what roadblocks or barriers may lie in the way of their destination, and so forth.

*Strategic Indicators for Higher Education** is a study that offers 100 indicators used as benchmarks by more than 1,000 public and private colleges and universities. Although not all the indicators apply equally to independent schools, there are clear lessons for schools in this book. Let's look at the Big 10 Indicators as adjusted for independent schools.

1. Revenue structure. What are the sources of your school's revenue stream? Have you become more or less tuition dependent? How stable and reliable have your patterns of income been in the last five years? What changes can you reasonably anticipate? What are the trends in your non-tuition revenue sources? Some scholars suggest the value of quasi-endowment is one of an institution's strongest signs of health. Unlike restricted gifts to endowment (for financial aid, faculty salaries, etc.), board-designated surpluses (or quasi-endowment) reflect the capacity of the school to apply present savings toward future needs.

---

* Barbara E. Taylor and William F. Massey. *Strategic Indicators for Higher Education: Vital Benchmarks and Information to Help You Evaluate and Improve Your School's Performance.* Princeton, NJ: Peterson's Guides, 1997.

2. Expenditure structure. What are the principal uses of and trends in expenditure? What changes are likely in the future? Many colleges, having seen financial aid grow rapidly in the past 10 years, are scaling back on these dollars as a percentage of overall expenditures. Some schools have reluctantly, but responsibly, come to similar conclusions.

3. Budget excess/deficit. What is the difference between current revenues and expenses? How long could you operate without additional sources of income? If you have incurred deficits, how have you dealt with them? Over-reliance on one or two sources to cover deficits is dangerous and can jeopardize long-term financial stability.

4. Enrollment data. What percentage of applicants do you accept at key entry points? What percent of those who are accepted actually enroll? Examine student attrition patterns. How, and how readily, are departing students replaced?

5. Student/faculty ratio. This statistic — oft-quoted by independent schools to reflect their individual attention and small class size — is also a measure of workload and productivity. How large can a class be without endangering attention to the individual student? How does it look when broken out by division or grade level, by subject, and by teacher?

6. Financial aid. As requests for financial aid from low- and middle-income families grow, schools should measure the annual picture in two ways: (1) aid as a percentage of total tuition and fee income, and (2) net tuition income (total tuition charged minus aid awarded). Changes over time merit thoughtful analysis.

7. Faculty profile. Schools need to keep an eye on their overall faculty profile. What is the percentage of beginning teachers? What percentage have five to 10 years' experience? Ten to 15 years? Fifteen to 20 years? More than 20 years in the classroom? Your ability to fund and achieve educational goals will be affected by factors identified in such a profile. It is also informative to determine whether full-time faculty as a percentage of all staff is increasing, decreasing, or holding steady. What does all this mean at a time when there's a national shortage of qualified teachers?

8. Demographics. What are the diversity indicators at your school? What are your marketplace factors, goals, and actual achievements in recruitment, retention, and advancement of students and staff of color? Have you examined staff gender balance and related compensation issues? What is the demographic profile of your financial-aid students by grade level, income, gender, ethnicity, and geographic distribution?

9. Deferred maintenance. What is your estimated maintenance backlog (even if imprecise) as a percentage of total plant replacement value? Schools that in recent years have chosen to focus on other priorities (such as financial aid, faculty salaries, and technology) can find this a disturbing figure.

10. Giving trends. What percentage of your alumni and alumnae have contributed to the school in the last five years? What percentage of parents? Try to imagine how a foundation or corporation would view such a show of support. Trustees must set the tone with 100 percent participation.

In many of these areas, schools will want to ask a corollary question: How do our data compare with those from our peer institutions? Data vary by region, school, and grade range. Although each institution must establish its own goals, comparing your strategic indicators with peer schools' helps inform institutional priorities. For trustees working in NAIS member schools, it is helpful to know that NAIS offers comparative data in a variety of areas. (To see the data, go to *www.nais.org/resources/statsonline*.)

Even if your school is not presently taking its own measure in these ways, try using these questions as the basis of an exercise at your next board meeting. Without collecting or grading their quiz papers, ask all trustees to answer these questions. The exercise should help move the group toward understanding how best to use the time and talents of its members as guardians of your institution's future.

PREPARE TO PLAN — AGAIN!

Once a strategic plan has been established, some boards add an extra year to the plan as part of its yearly assessment. This results in what is called a rolling plan. Even with these yearly plan additions, the best boards undertake a full planning process at least every five years. Other boards begin a formal planning process in the last year of the current plan.

Are we doing this again?

With the strategic planning process, it is not only appropriate to go around in a circle. It is mandatory.

The Planning Cycle

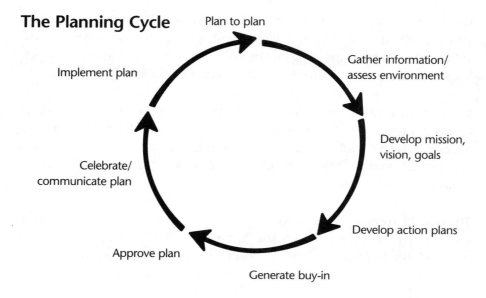

Plan to plan

Gather information/
assess environment

Develop mission,
vision, goals

Develop action plans

Generate buy-in

Approve plan

Celebrate/
communicate plan

Implement plan

Note: The accreditation process a school undertakes every five to 10 years provides an excellent opportunity to evaluate the school's total program, its administration, and its governance. The board should take ownership of preparing the governance portion of the process. In fact, where appropriate, trustees can serve on committees or task forces that are working on other parts of the planning process leading up to the report to the accreditation body. At the very least, all trustees need to be kept informed about the report, the visit of the evaluating team, and the report back from the accrediting organization. The board chair and other selected trustees will be asked to meet with the visiting team to discuss the governance section of the report the school submits to the accrediting body and perhaps other report sections as well. The recommendations resulting from the school's report and the visiting team's report can inform all aspects of the school's strategic plan and priorities. These recommendations should also be used to improve the effectiveness of every part of the school, including governance. Preparing for reaccreditation is time-consuming but worth the effort; trustees need to play an important role in the process.

As a trustee, you may be an active participant in the total planning process or in a section of it. You will examine the proposed plan carefully to be sure it contains a mission and vision that reflect the school's beliefs and desired program not only in the present but also in the future. You will also make sure that the goals will enable the school to fulfill its mission and achieve its vision and that the goals are viable. You want the school and all who serve it to reach for excellence so that its students will be productive, caring citizens who comport their lives with integrity.

DEFINITIONS OF PLANNING TERMS

There are almost as many planning processes as there are consultants. To say that this can lead to confusion is an understatement. The following definitions can serve as your guide to this chapter. After all, it's important that everyone involved agrees on the terminology when you and your school enter into a planning process.

Note: Not all boards require all of the following terms as steps in their planning process. For instance, some boards don't create both objectives and strategies. Others see no need for a vision statement or a philosophy statement. But a planning scenario must include, at a minimum, a mission statement, goals, and strategies.

The **Mission Statement** of a school describes why the school exists:
• What the school believes
• Whom it serves
• What it does

The statement should be succinct and serve as a guide to the actions of the board, administration, and faculty. A mission statement that truly captures the essence of a school inspires energy and commitment.

The **Vision Statement** (optional for schools) describes the school's desired future. It is an image of an ideal, an expression of optimism.

A **Philosophy Statement** (also optional for schools) expresses a school's bedrock values and beliefs about its educational program, students, faculty, support services, sense of community, etc. It often supports and augments the mission statement.

A **Goal** is a broad institutional statement of intent. Sometimes such goals are called policy or strategic goals. *Example:* The school will increase its non-tuition income.

An **Objective** describes how a goal will be achieved. It is concrete and measurable and can be assigned to a specific individual or group for implementation or accountability. *Example:* The annual fund campaign will increase by 5 percent each of the next three years.

A **Strategy** is even more specific than an objective and is often called an action step. Each strategy should delineate the following:
- Responsible group or individual
- Progress report dates
- Completion date
- Needed resources, both human and financial
- Approval authority
  - By whom
  - By when

Action Plans can consist of objectives and strategies or just lists of action steps. (For an example of how to diagram action plans, see the Action Plan form in this chapter's Sample Materials section.)

Yearly Operational Plans are one-year action plans derived from the strategic plan and from plans that keep the school going on a daily basis. Under the leadership of the head, the school's administration develops, implements, and monitors the operational plan. The administration informs the board of the status of the operating plan items that affect the school's ability to accomplish the strategic plan and any other activities that might rise to the board level because of a crisis, unanticipated major costs, etc. Boards should also adopt their own operating plans to bring focus to their work and to facilitate the assessment of their work.

The **Annual Budget** is based on the yearly operational plan.

CASE STUDY

WHAT'S THE PLAN?

Parents of students at Generation X Academy have become increasingly alarmed at the rift between the school head and its board. The head wants to steer the academy toward a closer alliance with local industry in an effort to gain corporate funding for large projects. But the board believes that establishing and maintaining a top-notch athletic program will bring far more revenue and prestige to the school. At meetings, shouting matches develop between the head and the board.

The academy begins to founder. Industry wants no part of a school in such turmoil, and elite coaches and athletes want clear evidence of a strong institutional commitment to athletics before they sign on at the academy.

What are the issues?
What should the board do?
What should the head do?
What should the chair do?

S A M P L E   M A T E R I A L S

ACTION PLAN FORM

Goals:

Action	Responsibility	Target Date	Resources Needed	Approval Authority	How and By When?

RESOURCES

Barry, Bryan. *Strategic Planning Workbook for Nonprofit Organizations.* St. Paul, MN: Amherst H. Wilder Foundation, 1997.

Evans, Robert. *The Human Side of School Change: Reforms, Resistance, and Real-Life Problems of Innovation.* San Francisco, CA: Jossey-Bass, 1996.

Grace, Kay Spinkel. *The Board's Role in Strategic Planning.* Washington, DC: BoardSource,* 1997.

*Formerly the National Center for Nonprofit Boards

Howe, Fisher. *The Board Member's Guide to Strategic Planning: A Practical Approach to Strengthening Nonprofit Organizations.* San Francisco, CA: Jossey-Bass, 1997.

Rouse, William B. *Don't Jump to Solutions: Thirteen Delusions That Undermine Strategic Thinking.* San Francisco, CA: Jossey-Bass, 1998.

Stone, Susan C. *Shaping Strategy: Independent School Planning in the '90s.* Washington, DC: National Association of Independent Schools, 1993.

. . . .
CHAPTER 5

ASSURING THE FINANCIAL STRENGTH OF THE SCHOOL

THE SCHOOL'S MISSION is your guide in all of your actions, whether you are planning for the future or developing policy. You are a steward of the school's resources — its people, its buildings and grounds, and its funds. One of the ways you exercise your stewardship is to ensure that the school has a secure, diversified funding base. As a school leader, you are among the first to contribute your personal financial resources. You are a trust holder of all that is the school, including its funds, and a model of giving for all to emulate.

Please note that this chapter is not meant to be a primer on independent school fund raising. For more information on fund raising, read NAIS's book *Philanthropy at Independent Schools,* 2nd Edition, by Helen A. Colson — the best resource on independent school giving.

THE NEED TO RAISE MONEY

Schools do not raise funds just for the fun of it; they do it to fulfill their missions and visions. Tuition at most schools does not cover the cost of

Why don't we just charge what it costs?

educating students and providing all the other services expected of independent schools today. Schools are facing demands to expand staff and programs, increase their use of technology for programs and administrative support functions, and, above all, to offer competitive faculty and administrative salaries. Unlike for-profit corporations, which are in the business of making money, schools must fulfill their labor-intensive, people-oriented mission of providing children with a good education. They cannot get more efficient by combining classrooms, reducing staff, or "firing" inefficient students.

Some schools depend heavily on tuition, especially K-8 day schools. Such reliance on tuition means that full enrollment is critical to ensuring that a school can carry out its program. The danger of relying on tuition as the school's sole income source is that the school may decide, for purely financial reasons, to increase tuition sharply or to expand the number of students. It would be better for the school to diversify its funding sources: annual giving, campaign dollars, endowment income, special-event income, grants, bequests and other planned gifts, and in-kind donations of goods and services. Think of a one-legged stool and one with seven legs. Which of these stools would give you the most secure seat?

I give my time. You want my money also?

Yes. If the board of trustees wants the school's funding base to be secure and strong, each trustee must play a role. The primary rule of fund raising states that you cannot ask for a contribution until you make one yourself. Why should anyone give to the school if the leadership does not give? Trustees need to make significant gifts, according to their abilities to do so, and make them at the beginning of any campaign. Board members also need to make the school one of the top charities to which they give. (If board members wish to make a pledge, that is fine. However, they need to fulfill that pledge by the deadline.) The current standard of board participation is 100 percent, and, increasingly, foundations and individuals will give only if the school can demonstrate that all trustees have given or pledged. The primary trustee role in fund development is to give.

PERCEIVED BARRIERS TO INVOLVEMENT IN FUND DEVELOPMENT

Trustees cite a number of reasons for their reluctance to ask others for money. The following are common problems and possible solutions.

"I don't know how."
Offer training and a buddy system through which trustees go in pairs (consisting of one veteran asker and one neophyte) to solicit a gift.

I'll do anything except raise funds.

"It's the responsibility of the head and director of development."
Go back and reorient current board members to their responsibilities. Also make sure that the committee on trustees tells prospective board members that they are expected to give and participate in fund-raising activities. No one should be appointed to the board until he or she understands and heartily accepts this role.

"I'll be asked to give a gift in return."
"Asks" should be done for the school, not as a favor to the person making the request. However, this tit-for-tat mentality does exist, and trustees need to think about how they might reorient such a response back to the commitment the asker and giver share for the school.

"I don't know anyone with money."
Often this is not true, but if a trustee believes it to be so, the director of development and development committee chair can work with the trustee to examine his or her connections. Perhaps the trustee could generate a list of potential donors by reviewing an address book, a list of parents from his or her children's class, etc. If after coming up with a list, the board member still does not want to make the actual contact, at least he or she will have participated in the fund development process and may be motivated to move into other development activities over time.

"I did it once, and it was a disaster."
Either have the trustee make thank-you calls to donors without asking for further gifts or cajole him or her into going with a seasoned solicitor to visit a donor who is sure to make a gift. The latter will give the trustee a taste of success.

"I just don't have the time."

Trustees need to see fund raising as a priority. Even those who have little time available can make one call per semester, especially if the development office is effectively staffed and can do the necessary preparation before the call is made. The trustees may also agree to do more calls if the potential contacts further other social or business interests of theirs.

"I don't understand why the school needs all this money."

Education is key here. However, if the trustee cannot understand the case for fund raising, she or he may be so disconnected from the school and the board that a more fundamental conversation is needed. It could also be that the total board has failed to fully discuss the school's critical issues, including the need for funds and the board's role in grappling with the issues by raising money.

See the Sample Materials section at the end of this chapter for a survey that can help assess trustees' readiness to raise funds.

THE ROLE OF TRUSTEES IN FUND DEVELOPMENT

What can we do?

Trustees can contribute to fund development through a variety of activities. After making personal gifts, they can offer an opportunity to others to support the school by contributing financial resources. In fact, board members usually assume leadership positions in fund-raising activities by chairing the development committee or other committees for the annual fund, special events, planned giving, and the capital campaign. All trustees should participate in development efforts according to their skills, contacts, and experience. The chief cheerleader of the board's fund-raising role must be the board chair. If the chair does not embrace this role, it will be very difficult to enlist other trustees.

Even though at times a head may wish he or she had a "fund-raising board," such a wish could lead to more money but also to a lack of understanding of the school's true mission. A head should really desire a "board that raises funds."

Trustees can be involved in a number of specific fund development activities as the school seeks major gifts.

• **Assessing prospects.** Board members can help the development officer or fund-raising leadership rate the capacity of an individual to give based on personal knowledge of the prospect.

- **Identifying and assisting in the cultivation of donors.** Even if they do not ask for gifts, trustees can speak formally or informally to parents, past parents, alumnae and alumni, and friends of the school. Trustees can also host events where the head can speak. Playing host can be especially helpful in locations outside the school's geographic region.
- **Opening the door for solicitations.** A trustee can schedule meetings for others to attend or accompany others to calls. The likelihood of success is higher when trustees make the initial contact and go on the call with the head, the director of development, or another trustee.
- **Making sure the case is a compelling match for the donor's interests.** This kind of inside knowledge is very valuable. If the donor's interests are unknown, those involved may need to make several visits before asking for a gift and even more before receiving one.
- **Asking for a donation.** Because their devotion to the school is so clear, trustees or other volunteers are almost always the most appropriate people to actually request a gift. Donors may perceive the head, director of development, and other staff as having a conflict of interest because their salaries may come in part from donated funds.
- **Thanking donors personally and staying in touch with them.** Attentive stewardship greatly facilitates the next request. Trustees can do a good job of keeping donors informed of how their gifts have supported the work of the school.
- **Monitoring progress.** At least quarterly, board members should monitor the amount of funds board members have raised and the percentage of trustees contributing to the annual fund or capital campaign.

A list of possible ways in which trustees can participate in board fund-raising activities appears in the Sample Materials section at the end of this chapter. This list can be used as a board-training tool.

REACHING YOUR FUND-RAISING GOALS

Beyond giving and getting, trustees must also:

> How does the board assure that the school will raise what it needs?

- Budget sufficient funds to cover the cost of fund-raising activities, including salaries for a director of development and additional staff, if possible. Development directors are among the most highly compensated school personnel. Never expect to pay them a low salary and then give them a percentage of what they raise. Because of the obvious conflict of interest it creates, this practice is considered unethical by all fund-raising professional associations and monitoring organizations.

- Work with the staff to create an annual development plan that takes into account current and future operational and capital needs and works in concert with the established goals of the strategic plan.
- Monitor the fund development efforts to assure that they are well managed and cost-effective and that the funds are used as promised.
- When the school sets fund-raising goals for budgeting purposes, satisfy yourself that the goals are realistic, not just a "plug" number to balance the budget.

TYPES OF FUND DEVELOPMENT ACTIVITIES

> I never knew there were so many ways people can give.

Even though this chapter is not meant to be Fund Raising 101, trustees need to be aware of all the various ways a school can raise money. In addition to being important general knowledge, it may awaken a trustee's interest in working on one of the activities, or it may prompt giving differently — or giving more. Here are the most common ways in which schools raise funds.

Annual funds in support of current operations may be solicited via phonathons, mail appeals, or personal visits. There are usually different levels of giving, with the greatest amount of attention going to prospective major donors.

Grants often come from foundations, especially family foundations. Foundations are increasingly likely to support schools' operating funds and special projects. Corporate foundations are less likely to give grants, though they may match their employees' gifts to the school.

Special events take significant time and effort from both volunteers and staff, but the right events can produce important dollars and reach people beyond the school community. They can be excellent opportunities to raise the school's visibility and bring new friends into the fold. However, a board needs to critically assess all events to make sure they're truly efficient and meet their established goals. Some may raise so little money that the return is only a few cents per volunteer hour. And if there are too many events, staff and volunteers will burn out or, worse, think they have "already given." Remember, the most cost-effective way to raise the most money is to directly ask individuals for contributions.

Capital campaigns raise substantial funds for buildings or property improvements. Campaigns may be intended for the construction or purchase of buildings, purchase of land, renovations, or to buy necessary new equipment.

Endowment campaigns raise major funds to increase what is often thought of as the school's savings account. Endowment income can relieve the operating budget and is often restricted by donors to specific areas, such as faculty salaries, financial aid, maintenance of buildings and grounds, and special projects. Some campaigns combine capital and endowment goals.

Note: A school should undertake a major endowment or capital campaign only after conducting a feasibility study with an outside consultant. A feasibility study will provide an objective view of whether a school should commit to a campaign, where support will come from, and what the financial goal should be. It is the board's role to establish a campaign, including defining its purposes and setting the goal.

Planned giving (also known as deferred giving) brings gifts from individuals, primarily through bequests, charitable remainder trusts, pooled income funds, gift annuities, and life insurance policies. For many years, colleges and universities have excelled at attracting planned gifts. It takes expertise to bring them in, but over time the effort can pay great dividends. Trustees may lead by example by working with the school to develop their own planned gifts and encouraging others to do so.

As a trustee, you contribute to attaining the goal of 100 percent board member participation in school funding campaigns as well as establishing a planned gift, if appropriate. Only you can decide the right amount to give, depending on your capacity, but you should make the school one of your top charitable priorities. You are a giver of time, talents, and treasure.

A FINAL NOTE ON ELEMENTARY SCHOOLS AND FUND RAISING

Elementary schools sometimes find running a fund development program problematic. Graduates of schools that range from pre-K to eighth grade eventually go on to high school, then to colleges and universities, and often to graduate school. Each of these institutions has a claim on the students' loyalty and may stand between the elementary school and its graduates. What's more, young parents, in particular, may find it difficult to give major gifts during their children's first school years.

These challenges notwithstanding, elementary schools need fund development. If your school has not already cultivated its graduates, undertake a program that either reconnects them to their first school or strengthens current connections. Schools that keep in touch with their young alumni, that invite them back periodically to school, and that establish a pattern of giving early (as with encouragement to "donate $20.03 for the class of 2003") inevitably have better results than schools that do not. Also encourage current parents to get into the habit of giving as early as possible and thank them warmly for whatever they contribute. Elementary schools can make a compelling case and certainly deserve their piece of the independent school funding pie. Some schools have found that a goal of 100 percent parent support, regardless of the size of the gift, is a good community builder. Of course, as is true in all schools, solicitation of major prospects generates the most funds.

CASE STUDY

A FUND-RAISING AUCTION'S PROPER PLACE

An urban school whose hallmark is a long-standing commitment to diversity uses an annual auction as its primary fund raiser. Last year, the auction generated more than $75,000 to supplement the annual operating budget. This year, the school's 50th anniversary, promises even greater revenues. The event normally draws from beyond the school community, but now the auction committee wants to provide even more community outreach. The committee proposes to move the auction from the school's gymnasium to an elite country club that is widely known to have restrictive membership policies.

The board chair notes that a board-adopted policy prevents the school from holding events in venues whose membership policies are discriminatory. But the event chair, a major donor, believes that because this is a special year, the school should hold the event off site. "This particular location will increase our visibility in the community," he insists, "and bring in a substantial number of wealthy prospective donors to the event, expanding our fund-raising potential."

What are the issues?
What should the chair do?
What should the head do?
What should the board do?

S A M P L E   M A T E R I A L S

HOW BOARD MEMBERS MAY PARTICIPATE
IN FUND DEVELOPMENT

- Make a personal contribution.
- Fully understand and endorse the case.
- Understand, endorse, and oversee the fund-raising plan.
- Contribute to the prospect/mailing list.
- Help identify and evaluate prospects.
- Share in cultivating key prospects.
- Make introductions to prospects.
- Write supporting letters.
- Write thank-you letters/participate in thank-a-thons.
- Write personal notes on annual appeals.
- Accompany others in asking.
- Ask for a contribution.

SAMPLE MATERIALS

JOB DESCRIPTION FOR DEVELOPMENT COMMITTEE
(ALSO KNOWN AS THE FUND DEVELOPMENT, FUND-RAISING, OR RESOURCE DEVELOPMENT COMMITTEE)

Responsibilities

The primary role of the development committee shall be to advise the board and staff of the school on all matters pertaining to fund development and to oversee and coordinate the ongoing fund development efforts of the school.

The specific committee responsibilities shall be to:

- Establish fund development goals and organizational structures.
- Approve the annual fund development plan (including the case statement, calendar, budget, goals, etc.) and inform the board. The board approves the goal as part of the annual budget process.
- Identify ways trustees can be involved in the raising of funds and match individual board members with the activities that complement their skills and interests.
- Identify and assist with the recruitment of the volunteers (including parents and alumnae/i) for the various activities.
- Assist in identifying major donors.
- Make contacts or conduct solicitations with major donors when a committee member is the right person to make such a contact.
- Advise on the community relations and communications plan as it relates to fund development activities for the year.
- Monitor the progress of the annual campaign and keep the board informed.
- Coordinate with the capital campaign committee (if one exists).
- Establish and implement a system of recognition for board and other volunteers who are active in fund raising.

Committee Members and Staff

Development committee members should be people who:

- Are committed givers to the school.
- Believe in the mission of the school.
- Are skilled in fund raising or willing to learn the skills to do the job.
- Are highly regarded by the school community.
- Are willing to give the necessary time.

The size of the committee depends on the amount of tasks to be accomplished. But it shouldn't be so large that the chair spends all his or her time facilitating meetings and other logistics. Seven to 10 members is the average. The development director should staff the committee.

Meetings

The development committee should meet at least quarterly. At times, however, the committee may need to increase the frequency to monthly or even weekly meetings. In addition, members should be on call for individual assignments. Boarding school development committees may need to use communications technology since meeting quarterly or more may be difficult and expensive.

S A M P L E   M A T E R I A L S

BOARD READINESS SURVEY
(Circle one response for each activity—and be candid.)

As a board member, I am willing to do the following:

1. Contribute	YES	NO	WITH MORE TRAINING
2. Understand the case	YES	NO	WITH MORE TRAINING
3. Understand the fund-raising plan	YES	NO	WITH MORE TRAINING
4. Contribute names of potential donors to the mailing list	YES	NO	WITH MORE TRAINING
5. Identify prospective donors	YES	NO	WITH MORE TRAINING
6. Make introductions to prospective donors	YES	NO	WITH MORE TRAINING
7. Cultivate prospective donors	YES	NO	WITH MORE TRAINING
8. Write letters and thank-you notes	YES	NO	WITH MORE TRAINING
9. Make thank-you calls	YES	NO	WITH MORE TRAINING
10. Make the ask	YES	NO	WITH MORE TRAINING

RESOURCES

Association of Fundraising Professionals (formerly the National Society of Fundraising Executives). Alexandria, VA. *www.afpnet.org.* Check this association's local and state chapters for workshops and materials.

The Chronicle of Philanthropy. Washington, DC. *www.philanthropy.com.*

Colson, Helen A. *Philanthropy at Independent Schools, 2nd Edition.* Washington, DC: National Association of Independent Schools, 2002.

Foundation News. Washington, DC: Council on Foundations. *www.foundationnews.org/.*

George, G. Worth. *Fearless Fund-Raising for Nonprofit Boards.* Washington, DC: BoardSource,* 1996.

*Formerly the National Center for Nonprofit Boards

Grant Thornton. *Planned Giving: A Board Member's Perspective.* Washington, DC: BoardSource,* 1999.

"Gifts That Give Back" (part of the Independent School Parent Series of booklets). Washington, DC: National Association of Independent Schools, 2003.

Schumacher, Edward C. *Capital Campaigns: Constructing a Successful Fund-Raising Drive.* Washington, DC: BoardSource,* 2001.

Weisman, Carol E. (Ed.). *Secrets of Successful Fundraising.* St. Louis: F.E. Robbins & Sons Press, 2000.

CHAPTER 6

DEVELOPING THE EFFECTIVE BOARD

A S A TRUSTEE, you contribute and ask others to do the same so that your school can fulfill its mission. You exercise your fiduciary responsibilities and monitor the use of all resources. Of course, a major resource of any school is the board of trustees. You work to assure the effectiveness of the board and the success of the school in future years by being involved in bringing potential trustees to the attention of the committee on trustees and by taking advantage of opportunities to develop your own board skills. You not only welcome board members from diverse backgrounds and perspectives, but you also celebrate such diversity because it opens a multitude of possibilities for the life of the school and board. You serve as a guardian of the school's well-being now and in the future.

THE IMPORTANCE OF THE COMMITTEE ON TRUSTEES

Each and every trustee is critical to the effective functioning of the board. If the board, in concert with the head, constitutes the school's leadership, then every board seat should be filled by competent and committed individuals who give of their time, talents, and treasure. If this idea seems self-

> After four meetings, I have never seen trustee Jones.

evident, then why do you find boards with many trustees chronically absent from board and committee meetings, unwilling to give or get, or just disconnected from the board's work?

A strong committee on trustees is not the only solution to problems of trustee ineffectiveness, but it is a major part. This committee, known as the nominating committee in the past, now plays a larger, more significant role. Along with the board chair and head, it can bring about and sustain a dynamic, productive board over time. In fact, the committee on trustees is the most critical committee of the board. No matter how experts suggest that a board should be organized, they all recommend that every board have an active committee on trustees (which may also be called the board development, governance, or nominating committee).

TIME COMMITMENT

> Isn't the committee on trustees a great one for those with little time to give to board work?

No. It is a year-round, hard-working committee whose goal is to assure the best possible leadership for the school, today and in the years ahead.

If the committee on trustees is so important, and if it is to be an agent of change, its members should be recognized by the board and school community as individuals who put the best interests of the school ahead of personal and professional concerns or biases. Some committees are elected by the board, but most are appointed by the board chair or by the chair in consultation with the executive committee. Most schools have only trustees serving as committee members, as trustees know the needs of the school and the board better than others who have not served. However, some schools do recruit past trustees, non-board parents and graduates, non-school leaders (such as educators from other institutions), or any combination of such people. The head and board chair should be active participants on the committee, serving as ex-officio members.

No matter how the committee is constituted, its members should exhibit the following characteristics:

- commitment to the school's mission;
- knowledge of the school — its program, problems, and leadership needs;
- knowledge of what constitutes good governance;
- visible, personal support of the school's fund-development activities;
- independence from board and school factions;

- willingness and ability to evaluate sitting trustees and potential board members fairly and candidly; and
- willingness to make contact with and interview and recruit new trustees.

Members of the committee on trusteeship should also respect, and be respected by, the other trustees.

RELATIONSHIP TO THE BOARD AND SCHOOL COMMUNITY

The committee on trustees cannot act in isolation. It must reach out to every trustee and other members of the school community for assistance in building the very best board. The committee cannot identify every potential trustee by itself; it needs others to open doors and often to make the actual request for someone to serve as a trustee. The board needs to be involved in setting the criteria for trustees through participation in an annual or biannual self-assessment and in strategic planning that defines the school's current concerns. These activities will define the skills and experiences needed to achieve institutional goals.

Can't we leave this trustee selection to the committee?

BYLAWS AND THE COMMITTEE ON TRUSTEES

The school's bylaws set forth who should serve on the committee on trustees, whether they are appointed or elected, what the members' terms are, and how the committee chair is selected. Continuity is one of the critical characteristics of an effective committee on trustees. This can be achieved by having two- or three-year staggered terms, with some members continuing and others leaving each year.

You mean all this is in the bylaws?

The bylaws also state the number of trustees on the board, how they are nominated and elected, what their responsibilities are, and how long their terms are. It is recommended that there be specified terms, with a limit on the number of terms a trustee may serve (two three- or four-year terms, three three-year terms, etc.). Bylaws often state that a trustee who has reached his or her last term must leave the board for one year before being eligible for re-election. This rotation brings fresh perspectives to the board's deliberations. However, it can be helpful to a school to keep a valuable trustee close to the school and invite him or her back after the year's hiatus. If past trustees are kept connected, they can be among the school's best advocates and most generous givers. (For more on related topics, see the section about renomination on page 100.)

PRIMARY RESPONSIBILITIES OF THE COMMITTEE ON TRUSTEES

Wow! This is real work!

A committee on trustees needs to meet throughout the year to accomplish all of its responsibilities. No longer is it appropriate, if it ever was, for the committee to meet two months before the slate is presented at the annual board meeting, ask if anyone knows anyone who could possibly serve, and then cajole friends to be trustees as a personal favor, guaranteeing that "you just have to show up for a few meetings." Service on the committee on trustees is a major governance role for trustees, as it truly shapes the future of the school.

A NOTE ON BOARDING SCHOOLS

Because its members are dispersed all over the country and beyond, a boarding school's committee on trustees will need to use modern communication technology. Although such communication can be expensive, it is worth the effort to ensure that the committee can accomplish its work in a deliberate and thoughtful manner. Keep in mind that, as a rule, a trustee who is committed to the school and its mission, and for whom the school is a top priority, will be more effective than one who has great board skills but little commitment.

FUNDAMENTAL TASKS

The following are the basic tasks a committee on trustees must perform. (See the Sample Materials at the end of this chapter for a committee on trustees job description.)

- Assess the performances of the board and individual trustees and of the environment. The committee will facilitate trustees' self-assessment of the board and of their own performance. NAIS provides examples of assessment instruments (go to *www.nais.org*, NAIS Resources, Governance/Leadership), but committees on trustees should only use such instruments as the starting point for evaluation and then adapt them to their school's unique situation.

- Assess individual trustees. This is only one of many examples that demonstrate how important it is for the members of the committee on trustees, and all board members, to keep discussions confidential.
- Conduct exit interviews with departing trustees.
- Review the school's strategic goals and major strategies to discover what skills, experiences, and relationships the board needs to possess today and in the future.
- Review the demographics of the current board. Examining the gaps in a grid of trustee demographics, skills, occupations, etc., can help the committee focus on the characteristics that the board lacks and should seek in new trustees. (A generic example of a board profile grid appears at the end of this chapter. However, each committee on trustees should add the characteristics that are especially important to its own board.) Ethnic, religious, racial, economic, and constituency diversity are, rightly, of increasing importance to boards.
- Provide a summary of the board self-assessment to the board.

ADDITIONAL TASKS OF THE COMMITTEE ON TRUSTEES

Develop and communicate candidate criteria and solicit nominations

- Develop a list of critical criteria for new trustees, based on a thorough assessment of the board's and school's needs. Keep in mind the oft-repeated Three *R*s of trusteeship: the ability to raise image, raise students, and raise money.

Can't we just be glad anyone will serve?

- Check out the criteria with the full board by mail or at a meeting. (This, along with the self-assessment results summary, will keep other board members informed on the committee's goals and will prime them to be the committee's partners in building the board.)
- Communicate the finalized criteria to and solicit names from the board. Consider asking for nominations from parents, past parents, grandparents, alumni, and outside community members in order to expand the pool of potential trustees. Make sure that all nominators use the criteria as the basis for suggesting candidates.
- Continuously add to the candidate pool and encourage trustees to be ever-vigilant in identifying potential board members.
- Ask nominators for specific information on candidates. Do they meet the criteria? Have they been effective trustees elsewhere? Are they strate-

gic thinkers? Are they team players? What strengths would they bring to this board? Are they willing to contribute financial support that's consistent with the school's expectations for trustees and their means? Can they commit the necessary time? Do they support the school's mission? Why do they think these candidates would make effective trustees?

- Consider seeking nominations from individuals outside the immediate school community, such as funders, educators, community leaders, etc., if the committee needs to locate certain expertise not found within the school community. However, NAIS counsels against nominating faculty, staff, students, or the parents association president to the board. In part this is because the board deals with confidential and contractual matters involving some of these constituencies. More important is the great need to fill the limited seats available with trustees who possess the resources to give and raise funds. For more on this topic, see the Board/Governance section of Frequently Asked Questions in the Resources and Statistics section of *www.nais.org*.
- Understand that the larger the pool of candidates is, the more the members of the committee on trustees can be assured that their selections will make the very best trustees.

Identify candidates for the board

Based on the criteria and nominating information, rank the candidates. By this point all candidates should have successfully passed three screenings: They should have the expertise your school needs, based on its strategic planning goals and priorities; they should be able to bring with them the Three *R*s of trusteeship (raising image, students, and money); and they've been observed in action so that the committee on trustees can feel confident they will fit into the board culture. To help with this last point, it is worthwhile to have a "tryout" system in which potential board members are invited first to serve on board committees and task forces.

If major gaps exist between the candidate pool and the criteria, renew efforts to increase the pool. Keep a record of all those nominated and their background materials so that succeeding committees can review them. A person who doesn't fit the current criteria may be perfect for the board in three years.

Boards in the process of considering potential trustees sometimes find themselves in the awkward position of deciding not to recruit an individual who was led to believe he or she would be asked. To avoid this problem, the committee should consider taking the following steps:

- Make it clear that no one is to contact potential trustees, even to ask if they are interested in being considered. They can always say no when and if the time comes.
- Undertake as much quiet investigation as possible to create a short list.
- Directly contact only those on the short list, making it clear at the outset that the discussion is exploratory and that the individual should not expect that it will necessarily lead to an invitation to join the board.

Cultivate candidates

- Establish a cultivation or recruitment plan for each candidate and recognize that not every candidate is ready to be a trustee the first time the idea is proposed. It may take one or two years to actually make the "ask."

> If we tell them everything, they won't want to serve.

- Carefully select the best person to make the initial contact with the candidate to ascertain her or his interest. Usually, the person making contact is the nominator, but it could also be the board chair, the committee chair, or a member of the committee. Remember that this is only an initial contact, not the actual request for board service.
- Send background (the board job description and requirements, the school's strategic plan, etc.) to a candidate once he or she has indicated an interest.
- Hold a face-to-face meeting with the candidate. The individual who made the contact, the committee on trustees' chair, and the head should be involved in the meeting. (Heads have many demands on their time and may not be able to attend. However, cultivating and educating trustees is one of the head's prime responsibilities.) This is the time to discuss time commitment, attendance, and financial expectations. It is entirely appropriate to share giving demographics. For example, you might say, "Our range of trustee donations for annual giving is from $1,000 to $10,000, with the average gift being $3,500 — which is, incidentally, the average trustee gift reported by NAIS statistics."

  Also explain the issues facing the school, the board's role in addressing them, and how the candidate could add value to the school and the board. Candor is critical; show respect for the candidate by providing full information. Recruiters are sometimes concerned that if they tell candidates the full truth, whether about the time and financial requirements or school issues, they will frighten them off from serving. It is better for potential trustees to decide not to serve than to feel betrayed after joining the board and learning the real story. Such a situation can even lead to an early resignation from the board. Schools need trustees who are fully committed; it is better for all concerned to discover that level of commitment up front.

Note: Face-to-face meetings such as the one described above can be difficult for boarding schools. However, conference calls could be a substitute if an in-person meeting is impossible.

Recruit nominees

After the committee on trustees agrees on the slate of nominees, the chair or the board chair should contact each nominee to ask him or her to join the board.

Renominate eligible candidates

> Don't we always re-up everyone for a second term?

- The committee should always examine each sitting trustee's eligibility for renomination to another term. If the leadership is committed to a high-performing board, the charge to the committee on trustees should include this as a mandate. The committee must consider whether each trustee has fulfilled all trustee expectations and added value to the board.
- Current board members who have not met stated requirements should be thanked for their service and not be renominated. However, you hope that no committee on trustees would be in this situation because the board chair would have counseled any trustees who are underperforming long before the renomination process begins. Such counseling should lead the trustee in question to either improve his or her performance or resign from the board.
- The committee chair should contact trustees who have been effective board members to thank them for their many contributions and to ask them to serve another term.

Note: Most boards today have finite terms for board members, whether for two three- or four-year terms, or three two-year terms, or some other formula. The bylaws state the number of terms for which a trustee is eligible. They also state how long (usually a year) a former trustee must stay off the board before being eligible for election once again to the board. However, often bylaws allow for officers to remain in office or be re-elected after their last term is complete. By this means, some schools finesse the "year off" provision for those whose expertise and contributions to the board should not be lost.

Undertake careful succession planning and nominate officers

- There should be a "board career" plan for trustees that assures that future leaders have the skills to perform the responsibilities they'll be asked to undertake. The committee should take great care to have an active succession plan so that at least one or two people could take over as chair, treasurer, etc., at any moment. The committee should know not only who will be the next chair, but also who will be the one after that. For purposes of continuity and communication, some schools compose the executive committee of officers, who also serve as the chairs of the various committees. Some schools also rotate the board leadership. One trustee may be elected to vice president of the board, then president of the board, and then past president of the board and/or chair of the nominating committee.

> Why shouldn't he be chair? He deserves to be after being on the board all these years.

- Regardless of the plans the board may have laid, all potential officers need to be carefully evaluated. Although automatic succession from vice chair to chair, or chair-elect to chair, provides continuity of leadership, occasional circumstances can arise where such succession would be damaging to the school and the life of the board. It is helpful to have an out in the bylaws to handle such a situation.
- Some officers may be sought for certain skills, such as financial expertise for a treasurer. But leadership qualities, commitment to the mission, ability to build consensus, and a broad knowledge of the school are critical for all officers.
- The selection of the chair is the paramount decision of the committee on trustees. The chair should be the model for all trustees to emulate and a person whom trustees, administrators, faculty, and parents respect. The chair must view herself or himself as the manager of the board, just as the head manages the staff. A chair must be committed to teamwork and to work collegially with the head. NAIS believes so strongly that the relationship between the head and board chair is vital that it sponsors an annual Leadership through Partnership conference for heads and chairs; its purpose is to share best practices in governance and leadership and to provide an opportunity for the relationship to mature.

The relationship of chair and head sets the example for board/head and board/staff relationships. If the chair and the head have problems with each other, disaster almost always follows. It is nearly impossible for board chairs to be fired, as boards appear to be willing to wait out a board chair's term rather then asking him or her to step down. This has led to a number of heads' resigning, much to the surprise of trustees, even though everyone knew the relationship was not a positive one. (For more information on the board/head relationship, see Chapter 7. A list of desired officer qualifications appears at the end of this chapter.)

Select members of the committee on trustees (If this is part of the committee's responsibility)

For more on this, see the sample Officer Qualifications Criteria at the end of this chapter.

Present the trustee and officer slate, as well as the slate of committee of trustees members, if applicable

- The slate, with bios or résumés, is sent to the board usually by a specified time before the annual meeting.
- Most often, a single slate of nominees is proposed. However, bylaws can provide a method to propose additional nominees beyond the official slate, with requirements for notifying the committee on trustees by a defined date and seeking the agreement of additional nominees to have their names put forward for election.
- The election is held.
- The chair of the board or of the committee on trustees contacts newly elected trustees, welcomes them to the board, and tells them when and where the orientation will take place.
- Sitting trustees are assigned to be mentors to new board members. The mentors should contact the new trustees shortly after their notification of their election. This relationship should continue for at least a year so that the newcomer has someone to turn to for advice and information on the underlying issues and relationships that are part of every board's life. All mentors should have similar or parallel agendas or topics to address with new trustees, though the manner in which they offer help will naturally vary.

Conduct board orientation

As soon as possible, hold a rigorous board orientation that delineates

Why take so much valuable time to orient new trustees?

- the school's mission;
- board roles, responsibilities, and performance expectations;
- the board's relationship to the head and the rest of the staff;
- the board's organizational structure and operating procedures, policies, and other major documents;
- information on the school's history, finances, fund-raising activities, program, students, etc.; and
- goals of the current strategic plan.

Mail the board manual before the orientation or hand it out there. (See the Sample Materials section at the end of this chapter for a list of suggested board manual contents.) Remember that this is a massive amount of material for anyone to digest. Do not expect new trustees to grasp all of the nuances of governance, the ramifications of the strategic plan, etc., at the orientation. It will take time and ongoing mentoring for trustees to be fully oriented. Remember, too, that a board manual cannot substitute for a live orientation. If it is very difficult to schedule a group orientation, the chair of the committee on trustees, the chair of the board, and the head, if available, should meet individually with new trustees who cannot make the formal orientation session.

During the formal orientation, the board chair and head should take leading roles; other appropriate trustees and staff should also be present. However, a long list of presenters can overwhelm trustees. Be sure to allow lots of time for questions. Many boards supply all new trustees with their own copy of this *Trustee Handbook* and suggest that they read it in advance of the orientation.

Encourage board development

As a means to better serve their schools, the best boards regularly pause to advance their own training and knowledge. Examples of professional development for boards include workshops on governance, often led by experienced outside facilitators; presentations on current issues and challenges facing the school; presentations on demographics, diversity, or technology; and joint meetings or workshops with trustees from

What do you mean there should be a line item in the budget for board development?

other independent schools. NAIS offers a variety of professional development opportunities. One of the newest is an online, customizable board evaluation instrument (offered in conjunction with BoardSource) that lets boards evaluate and benchmark themselves against other nonprofit and independent school boards. Another is the Governance through Partnership program, which offers custom board training on site at the school. For more information, visit *www.nais.org/events/events.cfm* or call (202) 973-9700.

Retain new recruits

The key to retention is to involve all trustees in areas where they can add value and in which they are interested. It is critical to include new trustees quickly in the work of the board, especially if they were recruited for expressed reasons. Other ways to keep new trustees engaged are to:

- Provide for their education or training by budgeting resources for it. Trustees' personal development will add to the effectiveness of the board as a whole.
- Make sure that board meetings seem worthwhile by always focusing on major strategic issues. The board should schedule sufficient time for in-depth discussions of these important issues, which then lead to decisions, whether by consensus or a vote. (See Chapter 10 for more information on board meetings.)
- Maintain a warm, open climate that welcomes diversity in individuals and their backgrounds, experiences, styles of thinking, etc. It is a responsibility of the board chair to be open, engaging, and accessible to all trustees.

Recognize trustees

> **Another plaque?**

Even though trustees say they care so deeply for the school they serve that they do not need to be recognized, do not believe them. They love recognition!

Plan a formal recognition for those who leave the board. Plaques are nice, but mementos that demonstrate personal thought are even better. Student letters or pictures can make great gifts, for example.

It can also be very helpful to keep a valuable trustee close to the school and invite him or her to rejoin the board after a year's hiatus or whatever timeframe the bylaws state. By maintaining a connection with past trustees, the school can keep them among its best advocates and most generous donors. Do this by:

- Considering a yearly award or honor for a board member who exemplifies the very best attributes of effective trusteeship. Do not give it to officers only.
- Encouraging the board chair and head to informally recognize trustees for board and personal achievements all during the year, whether at meetings, by notes, or through other inventive means.

Remove trustees if necessary

In rare circumstances, trustees must be removed from the board because of serious infractions of board policy, conflicts of interest, malfeasance, extremely disruptive behavior, breaching of confidentiality, etc. Board bylaws should include a removal process that protects the individual and the school. The vote for removal of a board member usually is two-thirds or three-fourths of the trustees present and voting or, in a few cases, of all trustees. It is hoped that the board chair would be able to counsel the trustee to resign before the formal removal process starts.

Conduct exit interviews

No matter how trustees leave the board — through retirement or resignation — exit interviews should be held in person or over the phone. These interviews should include the following questions:

> Why ask their opinion? They're not going to be around next year.

- What did you like about your board service?
- What didn't you like about it?
- What are the board's strengths?
- What are the weaknesses and how can they be improved?
- What are the school's strengths?
- What are the school's weaknesses and how could they be improved?
- What are the major issues facing the school (as opposed to the weaknesses) and how can the board address them?
- What do you know now that you wish you had known sooner?
- Is there anything else you would like to tell the board?
- Is there some way you would like to continue to work for the school after leaving the board?

A summary of these interviews, with individual responses kept confidential, should be shared with the board as a part of the committee on trustees' assessment process.

TRUSTEE DIVERSITY

> I'm comfortable with this board as it is. Why change?

Boards of trustees have an increasing commitment to diversity in their student body, faculty, and administration. But when it comes to their own diversity, boards often struggle to include trustees of various ethnic, religious, and socioeconomic groups. Because the board should be the model of moral leadership in this area (as in all areas), this should be a case of "Do as I do" as well as "Do as I say." If a school states that it is committed to diversity, its board should reflect and honor the pluralism of the school and its community. As noted in NAIS's Principles of Good Practice: Equity and Justice, "Schools have found that the process of creating and sustaining an equitable and just community requires commitment, reflection, conscious and deliberate action, as well as constant vigilance." (A copy of these principles appears in the Sample Materials at the end of this chapter.)

The following are some steps that might be helpful as you work toward a more heterogeneous board.

- Be sure the board chair, head, and chair of the committee on trustees agree that a more diverse board is critical to your ultimate effectiveness and that they will exercise strong, visible leadership on the issue.
- Hold a board conversation on the issue and discuss questions such as:
  - Does our board composition reflect the community we serve? Does it reflect the kind of community the school wishes to become?
  - Do certain constituencies lack a voice at the board table?
  - Are we missing perspectives that could expand our thinking in broad new ways?
  - How can we move beyond tokenism?

Note: If there are only a few people of color, or of a religious faith that is a minority population in the school, do not expect those members of the board to speak for a group. Expect them to speak as any trustee might.

- Develop a plan for change. This responsibility usually falls to the committee on trustees, but since that committee already has many responsibilities, this could be the perfect place for a task force organized to develop the plan and guide the board in its implementation. Outside consultants can be helpful because they have expertise in diversity and change issues and are objective.
- Take advantage of community leadership programs and professional and service associations, especially those that involve diverse popula-

tions. Such organizations are often willing and even eager to place their members on boards.

- Talk to community leaders and ask for their suggestions.
- Try to get a number of less traditional trustees at one time and assign mentors who are experienced trustees and committed to making diversity work for the board. Involve the new trustees quickly in board work in which they can contribute their talents.
- Once the new trustees are on board, truly welcome them and the new perspectives they may bring. Celebrate the fresh ideas, problem-solving skills, and resources that are part of your trustee team.

DEFINING DIVERSITY AND MULTICULTURALISM

Schools tend to use the word "diversity" to mean both "diversity" and "multiculturalism." This is fine, though it can be helpful to consider the difference between the two.

> What do we mean by diversity?

Diversity simply describes the various constituents of a group. It's quantitative. Most obviously, it is defined by race, gender, and culture (or ethnicity). On a more subtle level, it includes class, sexual orientation, religion, disability, and even appearance. But the list can be as varied as a school deems necessary and right. It is helpful to pause and reflect on the many forms diversity can take:

- race
- gender
- socioeconomic status
- national origin
- physical ability or disability
- ethnicity
- politics
- culture
- family structure
- sexual orientation
- constituency (parents, alumnae/i, faculty, students, past parents, funders, friends)
- geographic area of residence
- age
- marital status
- religion
- values
- mental ability

...and on and on

Multiculturalism is generally considered to be an evolving process. Although diversity is quantitative, multiculturalism is qualitative. It is the shift that occurs when we move from defining everyone by one cultural norm to understanding the value of multiple norms. To put it another way, a multicultural community is one that embraces diversity and that believes the community is stronger, more equitable, and more just specifically because of its diversity.

THE FULL RANGE OF CONSTITUENCIES

Should faculty and students be trustees?

When considering new members for the board of trustees, most boards focus on the constituencies these potential new trustees represent. In considering bringing in new members based on their constituency, you should be aware of the following.

- **Parents.** Day school boards tend to have large numbers of trustee-parents. Often K–6 and K–8 school boards are made up exclusively of parents. Cooperative school boards are by definition boards constituted solely of parents. Parents bring a deep personal interest in the school. However, they can be focused on the present, generalize from their children's experiences, and become more involved in operational matters. NAIS recommends a balanced board, with 50 percent or less being current parents. Such boards, experience shows, have all the zeal of parent-driven boards but less preoccupation with the present and more of a future-focused, strategic orientation.

- **Alumnae and alumni.** Day school boards of K–12 and secondary schools have more alumnae/i trustees. Often, a majority of trustees at boarding schools are graduates. These board members bring a spirit of gratitude for their education and are living examples of the fulfillment of the school's mission. Occasionally, however, they are so enamored of the past that they have difficulty adapting to and embracing change.

- **Faculty.** A small percentage of schools have faculty-trustees. This is not a recommended practice, but many schools with faculty on the board find that they are deeply committed to the school's mission and bring their educational expertise and knowledge of students to the board's deliberations. However, most boards look to the head for such expertise and knowledge. In fact, a major problem with having faculty-trustees is that it makes them their own "bosses," as the board oversees the head, who oversees the faculty. This conflict of interest can make things difficult. NAIS recommends that faculty members not serve on the board;

rather, they should be included on committees and task forces where their expertise will be of value.

- **Students.** Very few schools have student trustees, and NAIS recommends against their serving the school in that capacity. Not only are they not of age legally, but their general maturity can make it difficult for them to move beyond their particular experiences as current students. Nevertheless, there are ways to involve students in the work of the board without electing them to it. Students may serve on committees, meet with trustees as student leaders, participate in surveys about their interests, and so on.

- **Past parents and grandparents.** These individuals may constitute the best of all worlds for trustee service: They're committed, knowledgeable, and distant from current school issues. Grandparents may offer similar perspectives. However, past parents might need more in-depth orientation than those who are currently associated with the school.

- **Funders.** Although all schools hope that all of their adult constituents will contribute funds, it is not recommended that representatives of private and corporate foundations serve on the board. In fact, many foundations have policies that forbid employees to serve on boards of institutions that the foundation does, or may, fund. A perceived or real conflict of interest may arise when such individuals serve as trustees.

- **Friends.** Though they may require more in-depth orientation, these trustees can bring the most objectivity as well as needed expertise not found within the immediate school community. Educators, especially heads, often serve as valuable trustees, as they bring the experience of other independent schools or institutions to the questions under discussion. However, it is recommended that you not recruit the heads of schools from which your school derives students or to which it sends students.

Although constituent-based boards have been the frame of reference for independent schools in the past, contemporary thinking in the non-profit governance world suggests a new concept: visionary boards, where trustees are selected less for the constituency they may represent and more for the imagination, team-orientation, and strategic focus they may bring to the table.

OTHER IMPORTANT ELEMENTS OF AN EFFECTIVE BOARD

FORMER TRUSTEES

Should we seek the advice of former trustees?

Far too many schools spend far too little time and attention on former trustees. Ignoring them is a mistake. In many schools, the head and board chair send all former trustees one or two special updates each year and invite them to parties for former trustees only and special state-of-the-school briefings. In addition, some schools ask former trustees to chair the annual fund, auctions, other special events, or, in some cases, capital campaigns.

HONORARY TRUSTEES

In the past, many schools created special post-trustee categories. The motivation is understandable; the advice of former trustees with broad institutional memories can be invaluable. However, some schools have reported problems with having these honorary trustees attend board meetings, where their presence can often impede the work of the board.

Schools that have had success with former trustees serving in an honorary capacity should obviously continue the practice. Other schools should consider finding alternative ways to sustain contact and maintain good relationships with talented former trustees. One way is to form an association of former board chairs. It can function as an advisory committee to the school head by meeting once or twice a year with him or her. Such a committee is particularly valuable to new school heads.

ADVISORY COUNCILS

Advisory councils have been effective in some schools but troublesome in others. Problems occur when the council has no clear purpose or mandate or when the group sees its goals as differing from the board's goals. Ambiguity does not help a school reach its goals. Schools that have success with advisory councils should continue to use them. However, a school should think carefully before initiating one. The key concern is whether or not such a council would truly help the school achieve its goals. Will it add true value?

FINAL THOUGHTS ON THE IMPORTANCE OF THE COMMITTEE ON TRUSTEES

Whew! This chapter lays out an incredible agenda for the committee on trustees. But it is imperative that boards assure their own high standard of performance simply because that performance will be a key ingredient in the future success of the school. This is why the committee on trustees is so critically important.

As a trustee, no matter what your background or connections, you mentor new board members, making all feel welcome and valued. You listen attentively to your fellow trustees' opinions and honor their viewpoints. You are open to new ideas and present your own opinions with candor and tact. Although you take your board work seriously, you should avoid taking yourself too seriously. You look for opportunities to bring appropriate humor to discussions, recognizing that a little levity can ease tense situations — and that joy and laughter are important to the health of the school community.

DIMENSIONS OF AN EFFECTIVE BOARD

The following is a list of board competencies that make for an effective, well-functioning board. This is reprinted with permission from *The Effective Board of Trustees* by Richard P. Chait, et al.

1. Contextual Dimension

The board understands the institution's mission, tradition, and history, and the board's behaviors are consistent with institutional values.

2. Educational Dimension

The board emphasizes the need to learn, to seek feedback on board performance, and to provide the opportunity for trustee education and self reflection.

3. Interpersonal Dimension

The board nurtures the development of trustees as a group, establishes group goals, and consciously attends to the board's collective strength and welfare.

4. Intellectual Dimension

The board recognizes complexities, tolerates ambiguities, sees trustees as one constituency among many, and understands how different issues, actions, and decisions affect one another.

5. Political Dimension

The board respects and guards the integrity of the governance process, avoids win-lose situations, and accepts as one of its primary responsibilities the need to build healthy relationships among key constituencies.

6. Strategic Dimension

The board directs its attention to a few priorities or decisions identified as having strategic or symbolic importance to the institution.

CASE STUDY

WHAT'S PAST IS...OUR PROBLEM NOW

In a rush to fill a vacant board position, trustees at River Academy, an institution highly sensitive to its students of color (40 percent of the student population), hurriedly approved the nomination of Bill Smith, who recently expanded his sporting-goods business into River's surrounding community. During a subsequent trip to Bill's hometown, one trustee became distraught when she discovered that Bill was a former youth leader of a white supremacist group. The board's bylaws do not allow for a member's removal unless that member "demonstrates behavior detrimental to the well-being of River Academy or any of its students, faculty, or staff." Since his appointment to the board, Smith has maintained a very low profile, so he does not fall under the provisions of termination.

What are the issues?
What should the committee on trustees do?
What should the board do?
What should the board chair do?
What should Bill Smith do?
What should the head do?

CASE STUDY

SPREADING THE WEALTH

City Episcopal School was a leader in opening access to independent education in its region. CES prides itself on its job program, diverse student body, community service, and close faculty-student relationships. Long before financial aid became a national commitment, CES forgave a good deal of tuition income each year in order to attract a multi-ethnic, multicultural student body. Although the neighbors raised a few eyebrows at first, they soon grew accustomed to seeing CES's African-American and Native American students sitting together with white students at the local Swenson's or on the Riverfront.

The faculty, staff, and administration of CES take great pride in the way that all parts of the student body live, work, and play together. No one is more proud than Martha Brent, the school's head, who is a graduate of the school.

Not too long ago, three vacancies came up on the CES Board of Trustees. Though Brent had not included them on the short list of candidates, Board Chair Arthur Maxymillian notified her that Bartholomew Thornton, Sidney Hamilton, and Ellen Sandisfield would be the new board members. The nominating committee, he informed her, felt they would be of great help in the about-to-be-announced capital campaign. Because of its tradition of simplicity, CES had an extremely small endowment, fewer well-to-do board members than most of its competitors, and an increasing problem with attracting students to the decaying physical plant. Only a major campaign could enable the school to hold its place as a campus on which students would be happy and safe.

At their first board meeting, Thornton, Hamilton, and Sandisfield each launched into a tirade against the amount of financial aid that CES was granting to minority students, which they said only contributed to people's weaknesses, and against the number of minority students in the school. Both Brent and Maxymillian were caught off guard by this broadside attack on a policy that was at the very heart of CES. As the attack continued, they looked around the table for support.

What are the issues?
What should the chair do?
What should the head do?
What should the board do?

This case study is by Richard Barbieri. For more governance case studies, go to www.nais.org, click on Resources and Statistics, then on NAIS Resources, and then on Governance Case Studies.

SAMPLE MATERIALS

BOARD MANUAL CONTENTS

Board membership and calendar
- List of trustees with names, preferred addresses for mail and e-mail, preferred phone and fax numbers, short biographies
- Board and committee job descriptions
- List of officers, with titles
- Committee lists, including names and addresses of non-trustee members
- Calendar of board and committee meetings and any other meetings or function at which trustee attendance is expected — for the fiscal or administrative year

Organizational background information
- Mission, vision, and philosophy statements
- Short history of the school, including how it was established, major events, and individuals involved at critical decision points
- Description of the total program
- Description of the student body
- Strategic plan
- Most recent annual report
- Public relations material, especially those items describing the school's program and facilities
- Organizational chart

Bylaws and policies
- Articles of incorporation, corporate charter, and bylaws
- Board policies on conflicts of interest, attendance at meetings, indemnification/directors and officers liability, reimbursement for expenses, giving and getting, etc.

Administration/faculty
- List of administrators (with titles), faculty, and staff
- Faculty handbook (or where board members can access it)
- Job descriptions of key administrators (or where they can be accessed)

- Personnel policies, including evaluation process (or where they can be accessed)

Students
- Student handbook
- School student/parent list
- Two or three issues of the student newspaper

Finances
- Financial policies and procedures, including investment policy (or where they can be accessed)
- Budget
- Long-range financial plan
- Most recent independent audit report
- Annual fund-raising plan
- Periodic financial reports (if separate from minutes)

Minutes and issue descriptions
- Minutes of several board meetings
- Brief description of issues facing the school, especially those that involve the board

Resources
- Bibliography on trusteeship
- Local, state, or regional independent school associations
- National Association of Independent Schools
- NAIS's *Trustee Handbook*
- NAIS's Principles of Good Practice (for Independent School Trustees, for Boards of Trustees, for Equity and Justice)

Note: Obviously, not all of the above will actually fit in a three-ring binder. An accordion file can work well to hold much of the extra material. However, a binder for the items to which trustees need to refer most often is very helpful. And make sure it has a pocket big enough to hold the Trustee Handbook*!*

SAMPLE MATERIALS

COMMITTEE ON TRUSTEES JOB DESCRIPTION

Purpose:
The committee on trustees determines the composition of the board — identifying, recruiting, and proposing new trustees. The board also facilitates the board's self-assessment; plans for leadership succession; and plans for trustee professional development through orientation, training, and ongoing education.

Tasks:
- Review plan for the year.
- Facilitate board self-assessment and undertake other assessments or evaluations to develop criteria for renominating sitting members whose terms are up and for nominating new trustees.
- Check criteria with the board and enlist trustees and others to assist with identifying candidates.
- Review board recruitment materials.
- Identify candidates and make sure that there is sufficient information on each one so that the committee can make reasoned decisions.
- Interview likely candidates to ascertain their interest and to begin the education process.
- Develop a slate of new trustees, with back-up candidates for each vacancy.
- Ask chosen candidates if they will serve.
- Present slate of trustees to the board for approval.
- Plan for the succession of leadership, evaluate current officers, and recommend an officer slate to the board for its approval.
- Select members of the committee on trustees (if this is one of the committee's responsibilities).

- Orient new trustees and organize continuing education programs that enhance trustees' knowledge of their governance responsibilities, independent school educational issues, and the school's programs and needs.

Members:
As described in the bylaws

Relationship to the Board:
Works closely with the board chair, who serves on the committee ex-officio. Includes the board in the process, especially in the areas of assessment, development of selection criteria, and identification of potential candidates. The full board approves the slates of trustees, officers, and members of the committee on trustees, if that is part of the committee's charge.

Relationship to the Head:
Works closely with the head, who serves on the committee ex-officio. Seeks advice of head on all aspects of the committee's work. Head should be involved in and have a voice in the meetings with potential trustees and new trustee orientation.

Time Commitment:
Year-round committee, meeting X times per year

Resources:
- Board self-assessment tools
- Nominating grid
- Strategic plan
- Orientation information
- Bylaws — policies
- Diversity goals
- Board manual
- Trustee expectations

S A M P L E   M A T E R I A L S

BOARD PROFILE GRID

(Schools can create a grid or simply group board members by categories. The point is to get a visual representation of the board's profile.)

Name:												
Sex:												
Male												
Female												
Age:												
21-35												
36-50												
51-65												
Over 65												
Race/Ethnicity:												
African American												
American Indian/Alaskan Native												
Asian or Pacific Islander												
Caucasian												
Latina/o												
Other												
Profession:												
Arts												
Banking												
Business owner												
Civil service												
Corporate												

SAMPLE MATERIALS

BOARD PROFILE GRID

Education: Elementary												
Secondary												
Higher education												
Entrepreneur												
Finance												
Human relations												
Law												
Media												
Medicine												
Politics												
Religion												
Social services												
Area of Expertise:												
Administration — General												
Education												
Facilities management												
Financial management												
Fund raising												
Health care												
Information services/technology												
Legal affairs												
Media/public relations												
Nonprofit governance												
Personnel management												
Strategic planning												

S A M P L E   M A T E R I A L S

BOARD PROFILE GRID

Constituency:													
Parent													
Past parents													
Grandparents													
Alumnae/i													
Funder													
Other													
Additional Characteristics:													
Ability to raise image													
Ability to raise students													
Ability to raise money													

The above items are only illustrative. A board-member grid needs to be customized for each school. Sometimes it is most appropriate to select only those items that are truly critical for the board when the evaluation is being undertaken.

S A M P L E   M A T E R I A L S

TRUSTEE TIME AND FINANCIAL REQUIREMENTS WORKSHEET

Ongoing Activities	Time Estimates Per Month (Adjust for boarding schools)
1. Board meetings	
2. Committee meetings	
3. Fund raising	
4. Other meetings	
5. Phone calls	
6. Leadership positions (officers, committee chairs, financial campaign chairs, special event chairs, parent association chair, and alumnae/i association chair)	

Seasonal or Time-limited Activities	Time Estimates Per Activity
1. Fund-raising campaigns	
2. Special events	
3. Issue task forces	

Financial Activities	Estimated Costs
1. Annual campaign	
2. Capital campaign	
3. Special events or other fund-raising activities	
4. Hosting events for cultivation of donors, potential trustees, etc.	
5. Board expenses (if not reimbursed)	
• Travel	
• Meals	
• Lodging (boarding schools)	
• Child care	

S A M P L E   M A T E R I A L S

OFFICER QUALIFICATIONS CRITERIA

Criteria	Name	Name	Name
1. Committed to the school's mission and vision and goals of strategic plan			
2. Willing to assume responsibility			
3. Able to exercise authority			
4. Able and willing to make decisions, especially within group decision-making process			
5. Knowledgeable about the school			
6. Actively updates governance knowledge and skills			
7. Maintains big picture of the school			
8. Focuses own energy and that of others on policy issues			
9. Sensitive to cliques and power struggles, but is disassociated from them			
10. Delegates responsibility to others			
11. Works to develop potential leaders			
12. Skilled at long-range strategic planning			
13. Able to problem-solve			
14. Effective oral and written communicator			
15. Has basic knowledge of parliamentary procedure and knows how to preside at meetings			
16. Contributes and raises funds			
17. Works well with the head			

This form is not in priority order. It would be appropriate for a committee on trustees to set the priorities that apply to its school and to add qualities/qualifications that are uniquely important to its school.

SAMPLE MATERIALS

SAMPLE TRUSTEE/SCHOOL COMMITMENT LETTER

Dear Trustee,

As a member of the board of trustees, you are in a position to make a significant contribution to School X and its students. The vitality of the school depends on your commitment and imaginative and caring leadership. In fact, the future well-being of the school is in your hands. You and the other members of the board are trust holders of all that is important to the life of the school and, as such, need to be clear about your responsibilities. I am asking each trustee to review the following areas of personal commitment:

1. Attend board of trustees meetings held X times a year. Your presence is valued and your active participation is a critical component of board deliberations. Therefore, according to the bylaws, after three unexcused absences, it is assumed that you do not want to serve.
2. Serve on a minimum of one committee or task force. The work of the board is most often accomplished through its committees, and your expertise will help move the board's agenda forward.
3. To be an effective trustee, you must read and be familiar with material sent to you in advance of board and committee meetings.
4. Contribute direct financial support to the school. We expect 100 percent of the board to contribute to the annual fund and also to any capital or endowment campaigns. Your support tells other potential contributors that our board of trustees is tangibly committed as donors. Trustees serve as key resources for access to other individuals, foundations, and corporations where they have influence.
5. Spend a half-day attending classes in a class or division other than your child's. Visits should be arranged through the head's office. By experiencing the educational process firsthand, trustees become better informed advocates for the school as a whole.

Just as you have responsibilities to the school, you also have the right to expect that the school will fulfill its responsibilities to you as a member of its board of trustees:

1. You can anticipate a judicious and respectful use of your time. The asset of time is one of the most critical resources busy people such as you have. We are committed to using your time in a manner that will return value to your personal contribution. If we fail in our attempt, please let me know.
2. We will get important information — including meeting agendas, minutes, financial reports, committee updates, and reports requiring action — to you in a timely manner before each meeting. We will also keep you informed about any critical events or concerns that may arise between meetings. Please let me know if the format of our reports does not facilitate your participation in the board's work. Are they too long, too terse, or confusing? Can you ask the important questions that need to be asked from the information provided?
3. We will provide you with a thorough orientation to the board and the school and ongoing training and education to help you be the most effective trustee you can be.
4. We provide directors-and-officers liability insurance. If you were to be accused of

S A M P L E   M A T E R I A L S

SAMPLE TRUSTEE/SCHOOL COMMITMENT LETTER

wrongful acts committed while performing your trustee duties, you are indemnified against reasonable costs of defense proceedings, damages, judgments, and settlement costs up to $XX per occurrence. Wrongful acts covered include making errors in statements or mistaking information, making misleading statements or admissions, performing misleading acts, and neglecting or breaching duties whether proven or accused. It does not cover willful negligence or criminal activity.

5. Please feel free to contact me at _____. I do look forward to hearing from you, whether it is with questions or concerns on school and board issues or even with praise of school and board accomplishments.

The quality of School X depends upon a committed, knowledgeable, and involved board of trustees. I look forward to serving with you and accomplishing results that will make a difference in the lives of our very special students.

If you concur with these responsibilities, I would appreciate your signature of commitment. Please return one copy to me in the enclosed envelope.

Sincerely,

Jane Doe
Chair of the Board

_____

Signature of trustee

_____

Printed name of trustee

_____

Date

Note: This letter is meant only as an example to be adapted for your school. It's best to have each section reviewed to make sure that it is accurate for your situation. Item No. 4 concerning directors-and-officers liability insurance, for instance, needs to be checked against your school's insurance policy.

SAMPLE MATERIALS

NAIS PRINCIPLES OF GOOD PRACTICE: EQUITY AND JUSTICE

Schools have found that the process of creating and sustaining an equitable and just community requires commitment, reflection, conscious and deliberate action, as well as constant vigilance. These Principles for Equity and Justice provide the foundation for such a community by ensuring the inclusion of a diversity of individuals and groups in the many aspects of school life.

The school respects, affirms, and defends the dignity and worth of each member of the school community.

The school lays the groundwork for its commitment to equity and justice in its mission statement.

The school establishes, publishes, implements, and monitors policies that promote equity and justice in the life of the school.

The school supports the ongoing education of the board, parents, and school personnel as part of the process of creating and maintaining an equitable and just community.

The school ensures a bias-free environment by addressing issues of equity and justice in pedagogy, assessment, curriculum, and programs.

The school values each and every child, recognizing and teaching to the varied learning styles, abilities, and life experiences.

The school uses inclusive, bias-free language in written and oral communication.

The school distributes resources equitably.

The school adheres to local, state, and federal laws and regulations that promote equity.

The school provides appropriate opportunities for leadership and participation in decision-making to all members of the school community.

The school engages parents as partners in the process of creating an equitable and just community.

The school develops in its students a sense of responsibility for equity and justice in the broader community.

RESOURCES

Andringa, Robert C. *The Nonprofit Board Answer Book II: Beyond the Basics.* Washington, DC: BoardSource,* 2002.

Andringa, Robert C. and Ted W. Engstrom. *Nonprofit Board Answer Book: Practical Guidelines for Board Members and Chief Executives.* Washington, DC: BoardSource,* 2001.

Bailey, Mark. *The Troublesome Board Member.* Washington, DC: BoardSource,* 1996.

Chait, Richard P., Thomas P. Holland, and Barbara E. Taylor. *The Effective Board of Trustees.* Washington, DC: American Council on Education/Oryx Series on Higher Education, 1996.

Holland, Thomas P. and Myra Blackmon. *Measuring Board Effectiveness: A Tool for Strengthening Your Board.* Washington, DC: BoardSource,* 2000.

Hughes, Sandra R., Berit M. Lakey, and Marla J. Bobowick. *The Board Building Cycle: Nine Steps to Finding, Recruiting, and Engaging Nonprofit Board Members.* Washington, DC: BoardSource,* 2000.

Johnson, Eric W. *Evaluating the Performance of Trustees and School Heads.* Washington, DC: National Association of Independent Schools, 1986.

*Formerly the National Center for Nonprofit Boards

Presenting: Board Orientation: An Introductory Presentation for Nonprofit Board Members (CD and user's guide). Washington, DC: BoardSource,* 2001.

Rutledge, Jennifer M. *Building Board Diversity.* Washington, DC: BoardSource,* 1994.

Self-Assessment for Nonprofit Governing Boards Kit: User's Guide with 15 Questionnaires. Washington, DC: BoardSource,* 1999.

Slesinger, Larry. *Self-Assessment for Nonprofit Governing Boards.* National Center for Nonprofit Boards, Washington, DC, 1995 (User's Guide & Individual Board Member Questionnaire).

Wilson, E.B. *The Committee on Trustees.* Washington, DC: Association of Governing Boards of Universities and Colleges, 2001.

· · · · · · · · · · · · · · · ·
CHAPTER 7

THE RELATIONSHIP BETWEEN THE BOARD AND THE HEAD

AS A TRUSTEE, you are ever mindful of your shared responsibilities, especially in three areas: (1) to help shape strategy and set goals, (2) to maximize use of resources, and (3) to assure timely evaluation of the work of the board and school.

You understand that the trustees, under the direction of the board chair, work cooperatively with the head and that the relationship can succeed only in an atmosphere of mutual accommodation and trust.

The relationship between the head of school and the board members, collectively and individually, is one of the most important determinants of the institution's strength and success. Some of these relationships are formal and others, informal. But in both cases, it is vitally important for all parties to be aware of the appropriate guidelines and policies for interaction. A well-functioning relationship between the board and head is marked by mutual respect; frequent, open communication; and candor.

Note: Because the board chair has so many special responsibilities in relation to the head, this team is the subject of its own chapter, Chapter 8.

THE FORMAL RELATIONSHIP

HIRING THE HEAD

The head is hired by the board, collectively — not by the search chair and not by the board chair, although the latter signs the contract. The entire board extends the offer of employment, with all its joys and challenges, and supports the head in the important work of the school. Because hiring a head is the single most important action the board can undertake, it should be done carefully, procedurally, and not too frequently. (For the NAIS monograph on head contracts, go to the Resources and Statistics Section of *www.nais.org* and look under Governance/Leadership.)

The written contract

Modeling good practices, the board offers a written contract to the head that delineates
- responsibilities of the head,
- terms of compensation,
- the evaluation process, and
- the term of the contract and renewal and termination provisions.

RESPONSIBILITIES OF THE HEAD

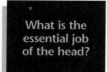

The responsibilities may be generally stated in the contract and amplified in annual goal setting or other supplementary documents. They should indicate that the head is the professional, institutional, and educational leader of the school, and that he or she is authorized to oversee all administration. The head serves in the same capacity a CEO would in a for-profit corporation (although some major differences exist between nonprofit and for-profit organizations, as noted on page 172 in Chapter 10). Other key concepts:
- The head works with board and staff to implement board policies.
- The head has complete authority for faculty, staff, and student selection, evaluation, and dismissal.
- The head keeps the board informed about decisions in all these areas.
- The head is responsible along with the financial officer (if any) and the treasurer of the board for developing and monitoring the school's resources.

COMPENSATION

Compensation should include cash salary, the basic benefits extended to all faculty and staff, and other benefits as the law allows and as the school is willing to customize them to the head's needs and wishes. The range of compensation covered in NAIS contracts includes insurance and pension contributions, housing assistance, automobile use, and vacation and sick leave, which can include sabbatical provisions. Other compensation can include covering some or all expenses related to moving, schooling for the head's children, club memberships and entertaining, and professional-development-related activities (memberships, conferences, etc.). Many heads also receive extra insurance and deferred compensation. In some schools, spouses have separate allowances as well.

Compensation review

Heads have different needs as individuals, as family members, and at different stages of their careers. Having expended great energy on the search and wishing to retain a person in whom the school has placed great hope and faith, the board attends to the head's needs by conducting an annual compensation review. This review is the responsibility of a small group of trustees designated for this purpose — usually the board chair and the treasurer, or the chair, the chair-elect, and the treasurer.

What factors determine the head's compensation?

To make certain the compensation they offer is competitive in their market, the members of this group avail themselves of national and regional research. (This research will also help avoid problems with the IRS, which requires that "highly compensated individuals" at nonprofits have their compensation determined by a documented process that benchmarks their salary against industry standards, such as the NAIS head compensation statistics. Learn more from the monograph on intermediate sanctions in the Government Relations section of *www.nais.org*.)

To assure a balance, the group also measures the head's compensation against that of other administrators and staff, both by considering annual "snapshots" and by charting trends in compensation growth over time.

EVALUATION

Working with the head, the board sets annual goals for both the head and the board. The annual evaluations then cover three broad areas:

1. the head of school;
2. the board itself; and
3. the board leadership, especially the chair.

Evaluations are based upon a small number of mutually agreed-upon goals set in advance of the school year and measured some months later — often in late spring, after school has ended. The evaluation process should be concluded before setting new goals for the coming year. Because the head serves as the employee of the board, the board alone should conduct the head's evaluation.

EVALUATION AND GOALS

The evaluation process must be based on mutually established goals and a mutually established process known and made clear in advance to all parties. The head's goals should work toward accomplishing the plan's strategic priorities for the upcoming year. It is important for both head and board to know what the focus of the year's work will be — the priorities and tasks will naturally vary from year to year according to where a school is in the cycle of the head's tenure, its capital campaign, etc. Of course, the board's own annual goals and work plans should also help accomplish the school's overall strategic plan.

Although the full provisions and details of the evaluation process do not need to be included in the head's contract, NAIS recommends addressing the topic of evaluation there. (The head's responsibilities could be addressed there, too, and perhaps expanded upon in a separate document.) Because the assessment process is so important, a new head needs to be informed at the start that evaluation of the head, the board, and the board leadership is a regular and ongoing part of the school's work. Do not say, "It's June; let's evaluate the head in some way." Goals and evaluation are the central measure of the head and board's work — too important to leave to chance, anecdotal reporting, or last-minute planning. Open-ended, 11th-hour evaluations that are not based on previously set goals are unfair to the head and to the school, and such evaluations are unlikely to advance its mission.

Compensation and evaluation

Some "experts" like to keep the discussion of compensation separate from evaluation, but in reality this is very difficult to do. Therefore, some boards tie a portion of discretionary compensation to evaluation.

Sharing the results of evaluations

The board chair should communicate the results of the evaluation in general terms with the full board in executive session. This is an opportunity for the chair to reflect on strengths and weaknesses and to indicate priorities for the coming year.

> How should the evaluation be shared with the board? With the head?

The chair and others on the head's evaluation committee, or as designated, should meet with the head to share more fully the overall results of the evaluation. It is appropriate that this group, or at least the chair, also meet with the head both before and after the executive session meeting.

CONTRACT TERMS, RENEWAL, AND TERMINATION

The head's contract should clearly spell out its duration. In today's world, the norm is multiple-year contracts, which can be advantageous because they offer stability to both parties. With a beginning head, particularly in the first year, a school may initially wish to extend a one-year contract.

> Should we offer a one-year contract or a multiple-year contract?

But in recent years, even new heads have been offered multiple-year contracts as they enter their positions.

The most common form of multiple-year contract extends for three years, with annual rollover provisions. By offering a multiple-year contract, a school indicates its commitment to the head's leadership for that period and perhaps beyond. Continuity is valuable, and such terms are a strong statement of support for a head. The expectation is that in return the head will honor the commitment for that term and stay focused on the school's priorities. In reality, however, sometimes heads get tempted by other opportunities. As a result, such agreements are, in essence, more binding on the school than on the head.

Renewing the contract

It is important to establish an annual timetable for contract-renewal talks, even in the middle of a three-year cycle. Compensation will change from year to year, as will annual goals. Because it is easier for a head to offer contracts to faculty and staff if the head's own contract and terms are firmly established, the middle of the school year is a good time to complete the agreement for next year's contract. Another common time is June, just after the evaluation.

Advantages of multiple-year contracts

Multiple-year contracts allow the school to retain a vital ingredient of strength and health: continuity of leadership. They let the head know of the board's commitment and willingness to work together. They also help protect the board from pressure by trustees who regard the turnover rate among corporate CEOs as a model and may urge a head to depart as soon as he or she makes the first mistake. In such cases, disaster often follows, usually with worse consequences for the school and board than for the departing head. Under multiple-year contracts cooler heads can prevail, the best interests of the school are more likely to be served, and everyone has the assurance that change, when necessary, is planned. (Another increasing cause for heads to depart abruptly: A board chair steps out of line in assuming the role of CEO and the board fails to discipline the chair as it should.)

Terms for the head's premature departure at the will of the board

Can't we just deal with this when trouble arises?

Everyone hopes that termination will never occur. Nevertheless, including a termination provision in every contract is important for both head and board. The best time to put the terms in writing is at the optimistic start of the new relationship. Unplanned departures can be disruptive to enrollment, faculty morale, community perceptions, and fund raising. A well-run and well-led board is unlikely to suffer this problem, and paying careful attention to many parts of this handbook will help schools avoid such an occurrence. But sometimes difficult situations do occur and, sadly, recur. They are easier to resolve when the terms are clearly spelled out well in advance.

At the first signs of concern about any aspect of the head's performance, the chair needs to discuss the board's dissatisfaction with him or her, and then the head must have the opportunity to improve. If improvement does not come about, the decision not to renew the head's contract must be made by the total board, not a subset such as the executive committee.

Termination provisions should be put in writing for several reasons, all of which offer protection to the head, the board, and the broader school community. Imagine a board that would let a head go without a departure package, not for cause but because the board decided late in the year to seek new leadership. By failing to act professionally, the board risks being unable to attract strong, committed candidates. Who would want to go to a school that treated its last head like that? A hasty, unplanned, uncompensated departure may also result in a qualified accreditation report. A school that does not follow best practices, even in one of the worst of situations, is probably not living up to its own mission statement or its claims about how the school values and treats members of its community.

Written terms will also help a school protect its own interests, especially financial ones. Three-year contracts are not commitments to compensate for three years if the board must ask the head to leave before that period ends. Multiple-year contracts usually stipulate that the board may give 18 months' notice before January 1 of the present school year, or 12 months' notice before July 1 of the present school year, that the school is not renewing the contract. A head then has reasonable time to seek new employment given the realities of the head search cycle.

However, if the board gives notice after January 1 — that is, after the date when many searches at other schools are well advanced or complete — the agreement should include a full year's salary and other benefits, as determined in compensation for the unplanned termination.

Heads are responsible for giving adequate advance notice of departure as well. A year's notice gives the school ample time to launch and complete a successful search. Ordinarily, a head who leaves voluntarily before completing a multi-year contract does not receive compensation for any time under contract that he or she does not serve.

Announcing the head's impending departure

The head and board chair should issue a joint written announcement to the school community. It should contain:

- The thanks of the board for all the contributions the head has made to the school and the plan for celebrating these contributions later in the year.
- The recognition by the head that the school priorities have changed since he or she was hired and that the head and board have agreed to part on positive terms.
- The commitment by the board to include the school community in the search process for the new head.

If either party demonstrates animosity toward the other or shares confidential discussions with anyone not involved directly in the process, the school will be greatly damaged.

A final word about the head's contract and compensation

Board discussions about a prospective head's contract and compensation, as well as about annual evaluations once the head is hired, take place in an executive session. Everyone who is not a voting board member is excused from the meeting. Only the basic parameters of the contract and compensation need to be shared. The chair could say, "We have extended the head's contract through the year 2006, subject to annual review of performance, to include a raise in salary within the 4- to 6-percent guidelines for all faculty and staff." Other details, including the actual terms of salary and benefits, need only be known to a smaller group of trustees who make up the head's compensation committee. Normally the chair, treasurer, and perhaps the chair-elect are the members of the compensation committee.

As a trustee, you understand that clearly stated basic terms and expectations in each of these four categories (compensation, evaluation, contract renewal, and contract termination procedures) are the backbone of a good contract and provide the foundation for a solid relationship with the head.

OTHER REASONS FOR EXECUTIVE SESSIONS

Are there other occasions when the board should meet alone?

Executive sessions that include the head may take place when sensitive matters are under discussion, such as potential real estate purchases, personnel policy changes, or changes in mission focus. Some boards take this idea further by adopting the model used by other nonprofits (especially colleges and universities) and having the board meet in executive session without the head at the end of every meeting. Such sessions last for no more than 15 minutes, and often less.

But many people, especially a large number of heads, are very uncomfortable with this exclusionary practice. A board that does this should ask itself why trustees cannot discuss difficult questions with the head present, even if the issue under discussion concerns a decision the head made. If the board cannot communicate openly and candidly when the head is in the room, the relationship is broken in some way and needs to be addressed by head and board together.

AREAS IN WHICH FORMAL AND INFORMAL RELATIONSHIPS OVERLAP

Other relationships that may arise between individual trustees and the head are delineated in NAIS's Principles of Good Practice for Trustees (which are distinct from the Principles of Good Practice for Boards of Trustees — to review both sets, see pages 23-24 in Chapter 1). The principles below cover the many areas that fall in the middle of formal and informal relationships between trustees and the school head.

SIX PRINCIPLES OF GOOD PRACTICE FOR TRUSTEES

1. An individual trustee does not become involved in specific management, personnel, or curricular issues.

From time to time, individual trustees may naturally wish to share their opinions with the head. Perhaps they want to talk about their perceptions of a student who's applying for admission, or offer the view that Spanish rather than French is the right language for 21st-century elementary students to learn, or mention that the soccer coach seems to be losing interest in her job. The key words here are *share opinions* — not *get involved*.

Once individual trustees have shared their thoughts with the head, the issues should be referred to the proper committee for resolution. For example, the faculty and the board committee on education may wish to hear more about the Spanish-French topic. But no matter what, the final decision lies with the school and its professional educators. The same concept should underlie all admission, evaluation, and dismissal decisions concerning either students or staff.

Note: An independent school's board should not act as a court of review or a court of last resort in discipline, dismissal, or termination cases. The first time the board acts as a grievance committee and overrules the head's decision is the last time the head will have any credibility within the school community. The board chair, who is the proper disciplinarian of the board, should speak to a trustee whose agenda is overly full of advice in these areas. Acting as disciplinarian is not a role for a head to undertake, nor is it the head's responsibility.

2. A trustee accepts and supports board decisions and respects board confidentiality.

Support for decisions

What if I disagree with a board decision?

The board can operate only as a collective entity: one board, one decision, and one voice. This precept does not mean that trustees cannot disagree in the course of researching, debating, and making decisions. Strong boards include people of different perspectives who will regularly consider alternative points of view with courtesy.

Nevertheless, after discussion and debate are complete, all trustees are expected to support the resulting decisions. If they cannot — for example, if a military school or a single-sex school decides to change its mission and several graduates cannot support that decision — then they should resign from the board. Resignations should be accepted with gratitude and understanding. At a later date, the former trustee may be just the person to return to the board after having time to see the effects of the new decision in action. But to have a trustee stating views contrary to the board's official decision is invariably damaging as the school goes forward on its new course.

Similarly, if a board reviews the head's performance and decides to put firm goals in place for the coming year so the head will have time to address perceived weaknesses, every trustee is obligated to keep details of the agreement confidential and to give the head support, both public and private, as the school moves forward. Again, the proper response for a trustee who cannot give such support is to resign. But even then, confidentiality must be maintained.

Confidentiality

We live in a culture that in many ways does not respect confidentiality. Our schools are not immune to the expectation that everyone can and should know everything. Especially in day schools, with so many current parents in the immediate community and on the board, there is a natural tendency to share confidential topics with spouses or partners. A good board chair will help work against this tendency with frequent reminders of the need for confidentiality. These reminders should begin during new-trustee orientation and continue when sensitive matters become the subject of board dialogue. Before discussing board matters with another individual, trustees should always ask themselves, "Does this person have a need to know what I know?" The answer, almost invariably, is no.

3. A trustee takes care to separate the interests of the school from the interests of a particular child or constituency.

Trustees may often be tempted to lobby on behalf of "third-grade parents" or "graduates from the '70s." But trustees should also remember that once they join the board, they speak for all constituencies, not a particular one.

Don't trustees get special privileges?

Trustees may also be tempted to lobby for admission or employment of someone to whom they are connected. These impulses are natural, and a wise head expects them. But having made the case for a candidate, trustees should leave the decision to the institution and respect even the decisions that are hardest to swallow. A trustee whose child, after due process, has been suspended or expelled from school may be tempted to leave the board or to withdraw a campaign pledge. But it is also possible that the trustee may agree with the process and the decision and will want to continue to support the school.

Similar logic is necessary when a school must deny a place to the child of a trustee. The trustee must have confidence in the admission policies and process, knowing that qualified members of the school community have determined that the child will not thrive there and deserves a more appropriate placement.

4. A trustee has the responsibility to support the head and to demonstrate that support within the community.

When trustees have concerns about decisions affecting their own families or close friends, or when they fundamentally disagree with a broad policy, they should express their concerns privately to the head, the chair, or both. Nevertheless, trustees should continue to give public support across the board.

Disagreement with the head

What happens when I disagree with the head?

It is not unusual for school constituents to initiate informal gripe sessions on the golf course, at the checkout counter, or in car-pool lines. A trustee may be tempted to join in, saying, "Yeah, I don't like what the head did in that case either, but...." To overcome this temptation, it may help to plan a routine response for all occasions and simply state, "The board relies upon the head's judgment in such matters, since our focus is strategic, not operational. I recommend you see the head to discuss this if you continue to feel strongly about it." As a head who was consulted about one of his most promising young administrators, a candidate to head another independent school, said to the faculty trustees of the prospective school: *"I expect you to support him when he is right — and also when he is wrong."*

Trustees themselves may sometimes wish to buttonhole the head with personal concerns. It can be tempting to approach a head at the end of a long day, perhaps even at the end of a long evening board meeting, to seek special help or a favor for a child. But in cases like this, trustees should remind themselves which hat they are wearing. You attend the board meeting as a trustee, not as a parent. A wise head we know, when faced with a request to reconsider a decision about a trustee's child at 10:30 one night, came up with a response she now uses regularly: "I know you want to speak with me as a parent, and I want to hear you out when I can give you my full attention. But tonight you are here as a trustee, and we focus on board matters. Why don't you call me first thing tomorrow, and we'll find a time to talk about this family situation as soon as possible?" In addition to helping defuse a potentially volatile issue, such a diplomatic statement reminds trustees of the different roles that members of a school community must play at different times.

5. A trustee accepts the responsibility to support the head and to work through established channels to resolve differences.

There may be times when one or more trustees has a concern about what a head is doing or not doing, or how or when he or she is doing it. They may disagree with a proposal the head has been testing or take issue with any number of other things. In these cases, it is critically important for trustees to adhere to the school's policies and procedures. Speak directly with the head or, if you feel you can't discuss the matter with him or her, talk directly and only with the board chair. You can expect a timely answer. In the interim, do not discuss the issue with anyone.

Throughout this period, remember that no head comes into the job with all the necessary skills and experience to lead your school. It takes time and a certain amount of trial and error. Your job as trustee is to help a head learn not to make the same mistake twice.

As a trustee, you know that your job is to help the school see what kinds of people can help the head be most effective in every arena. As a trustee, you know that your job is to give support when right and when wrong, even when the decision is reached that it is time for the head to leave.

6. Authority is vested in the board as a whole. A trustee who learns of an issue is responsible for bringing it to the head or the board chair and must not deal with the situation individually.

Naturally, members of the school community are aware of trustees' identities and will bring to their attention all manner of tales — important facts, unimportant facts, distorted facts, half-truths, and rumors. The board chair and head should regularly make it clear that there is only one proper response from a trustee: "I appreciate your sharing this with me and hope you will either share your concern directly with the person you have named [such as a teacher] or with the appropriate administrator." The trustee should also report this contact to the head or board chair.

> **What is the proper channel for complaints from constituents?**

Channels of communication made clear
The school should spell out the proper channels of communication in the faculty and student handbooks, in written communications with the faculty, and by any other appropriate means. Unless the school has a different policy, whenever an individual seeks the aid of a particular trustee, that trustee should state clearly that he or she will share the matter with the head and/or the board chair only but will not take up the individual's cause. The preferred contact is the head in most cases, but if the concern is about the head, the board chair should be the only one contacted. One of the many things head and chair should be sharing in their regular conversations, as we'll see in the next chapter, is the general trend and tenor of communications like these, even if there proves to be no substance to the reports.

As a trustee, you understand that no single trustee, even the chair, has any more power than another trustee, and no trustee can speak for the entire board unless specifically authorized — as in "the treasurer will meet with the auditor for the purpose of authorizing the designated transfers of funds to unrestricted endowment."

THE INFORMAL RELATIONSHIP

Invariably, many informal relationships develop between board members and the head — relationships that can be quite varied and complex. These offer many opportunities: to collaborate on goals and interests of priority to the school, to have a good time working together to meet these goals, to share in the joy of helping children and their teachers learn and work in a positive environment. In some cases, head and trustees will develop long-term friendships, especially if all remain aware that as long as one of the parties serves as a trustee, he or she is the other person's employer.

In the most general sense, community perceptions about some of these informal relationships may hold potential problems for the school and for the trustees as well as the head, whether personal friendships develop or not. By anticipating some areas in which common problems and misunderstandings can arise, you can develop your own strategies to avoid them.

"GETTING TO KNOW YOU"

Heads today find they spend more and more time getting to know each trustee as an individual, perhaps even formalizing the relationship by scheduling a one-on-one lunch at least annually.

Time-consuming as they may be, such meetings help the head get to know each trustee's particular interests and concerns. Heads today need the perspectives, experience, and talent of a variety of people in the broader world. Individual trustees can be valuable resources in that regard.

When the head spends time with each trustee, the trustee feels that his or her ideas are valued even if most of them do not reach the boardroom for a vote. Although there are obvious fund-raising advantages to such knowledge, there is also no doubt that the school's broader interests are well served when the head can identify and tap into trustee interests. New trustees in particular feel welcomed to the school and to the leadership circle when they receive such individual attention.

Some heads now spend more than a third of their time with their trustees, especially at schools in major fund-raising modes. Other members of the school community, especially faculty, may resent this, but it is time well spent. And it can be fun!

In summary, the individual trustee at his or her best helps the head and the school focus on strategic issues and assures regular opportunities to evaluate progress. The individual trustee follows clear procedures for communicating with the head. The individual trustee also understands the many responsibilities involved in supporting the head, especially in public, and appreciates the complex challenges today's heads face in leading a school.

FINAL THOUGHTS

In closing, it may be instructive to reflect on the wisdom of a famous head who was sought after as a trustee by many other schools and nonprofits:

> The final and most dangerous pitfall in the process of choosing a head is to think that the wedding is the goal, when in fact it is the marriage. No new head turns out to be any more perfect than any new bride or groom. Making the marriage work takes effort on everyone's part.

Making the marriage work — keeping the head (and head's family) feeling well supported through good times and bad, through successes and mistakes — this is a part of the work of every trustee.

CASE STUDY

COPING WITH AN INSIDE CANDIDATE

The current head has announced his resignation, so the Valley School has entered into a search process this fall. The search committee's charge is to bring its best choice for the next head of school to the board by January, if possible. A popular and charismatic in-house administrator has applied for the position. Although the board doesn't want her for the job, she is added to the finalist pool out of respect.

During the fall, the administrator wages an ambitious campaign on her own behalf with all of the school's important constituents — parents, students, alumni, and especially faculty. She even implies that after she is hired there will be conse-quences for those faculty who do not support her candidacy! The board ignores her politicking and narrows its finalists' pool to three people, including Ms. Administrator. After the finalists are announced, one withdraws to go to another school. The board offers the head's job to the other outside candidate, who visits the school and accurately reads the brewing situation. The outside candidate withdraws from the search.

What are the issues?
What should the board do?
What should the board chair do?
What should the head do?

CASE STUDY

CONFRONTING A DIFFICULT CLASSROOM PROBLEM

Meadowvale School is a relatively new K-8 school. Families identify with its distinctive educational philosophy, which is far less traditional than that of its cross-town rival, Greendale Country Day.

The students in Meadowvale's second-grade class have been difficult since the first months of their kindergarten year. However, by second grade, the students are older and more visible, and their lack of self-control is even more obvious to teachers and parents. Their teacher is Marcia Harmon, an experienced and respected teacher whose discipline style contrasts sharply with that of the relatively new first-grade teacher and of the equally inexperienced kindergarten head. The kindergarten teacher had provided a warm and home-like environment, and the first-grade teacher used her youthful personality to engage students in a personal relationship based on loyalty to her. Now Marcia insists that the children learn to obey classroom rules and respond to all teachers with equal respect. She believes that her charges need to understand that actions have consequences and that her response to misbehavior will be immediate and consistent.

In early October, the discipline issues boil over. Parents perceive Marcia as punitive; she finds bewildering their lack of support for holding the children to reasonable expectations. Despite several meetings among Marcia, veteran head Karen Harvey, and the concerned parents, the families continue to call with complaints. Marcia and Karen agree that although children often have trouble adjusting to second grade, in 12 years together they have never seen anything like this.

During late fall and into the winter, board members hear regularly from parents at school and social events but are reluctant to bring up the issue in full board meetings. In addition to being a veteran teacher, Marcia is married to the educational policy committee chair, Wilson Harmon.

In the spring, the issue comes formally to the board's attention when one second-grader's parents send a thick packet of material to each board member. The materials detail their correspondence with Karen and announce that because they have lost confidence in her judgment, they are withdrawing their second-grader and their kindergartner at the close of the school year. The head must also tell the board that three other second-grade families have failed to return their re-enrollment contracts.

What are the issues?
What should the board do?
What should the chair do?
What should the head do?

This case study is by Richard Barbieri. For more governance case studies, go to www.nais.org, click on Resources and Statistics, and then on Governance Case Studies.

RESOURCES

SEMINARS AND WORKSHOPS

NAIS offers the following institutes each year. For information about dates and times, call (202) 973-9700 or visit *www.nais.org/events/events.cfm/*.

Leadership through Partnership. This NAIS workshop gives board chairs and school heads an opportunity to reflect on their own working relationship together with colleagues from other schools. Between 60 and 100 schools participate. It takes place annually one weekend in September or October.

Governance through Partnership. This customized workshop for school administrators and their board members is held on the participating school's campus. A NAIS-trained facilitator (typically a current or former head or trustee) works with the school to tailor the length and focus of the program to individual needs. Schools requesting the workshop are asked first to conduct the online NAIS/BoardSource evaluation of their board to provide feedback to and direction for the board.

Institute for New Heads. This five-day conference brings colleagues together to learn about school leadership at a critical early stage in their tenure. Lectures, seminars, one-on-one sessions, and discussion groups with resident and visiting experts provide important perspectives on key educational issues. The institute also helps heads develop personal strategies to complement their own management styles as they develop an entry plan for their first months on the job. This is held annually in July.

BOOKS

Gale, Robert L. *Leadership Roles in Nonprofit Governance.* Washington, DC: BoardSource,* 2003.

Pierson, Jane and Joshua Mintz. *Assessment of the Chief Executive: A Tool for Governing Boards and Chief Executives of Nonprofit Organizations.* Washington, DC: BoardSource,* 1999.

Simmons, Karen and Gary J. Stern. *Creating Strong Board-Staff Relationships.* Washington, DC: BoardSource,* 1999.

*Formerly the National Center for Nonprofit Boards

> **"** A true team both
> defines its objectives and
> finds ways to meet them. **"**
> — Sally Helgensen

CHAPTER 8

THE RELATIONSHIP BETWEEN THE BOARD CHAIR AND THE HEAD

A S THE CHAIR OF THE BOARD, you understand that there is no more important factor in the success of the school than the relationship between the chair and head of school. You make central to your beliefs and actions the knowledge that together these individuals share — and model — leadership and governance and determine all that follows.

As is true of the relationship between the head and all trustees, here, too, there are both formal and informal roles, responsibilities specific to head and chair, and responsibilities that are shared. It is therefore critical that the chair and head make every effort to establish a solid and mutually supportive relationship of candor and trust, develop the capacity to be mutually critical, and learn from each other's feedback — all with the goal of making their work on behalf of the school most effective.

RESPONSIBILITIES OF THE CHAIR IN RELATION TO THE BOARD

- The chair takes the lead in areas of board leadership and management. The head, serving as the equivalent of a CEO, takes the lead in curricu-

lum, school operations, etc. Together they model the leadership relationship in action.

- The chair speaks for the board unless the task is delegated to someone else for a specific purpose. The chair is wise to let the head speak on behalf of the school on most occasions.
- The chair is the ultimate authority, along with the rest of the trustees.
- The chair serves as the leader and manager of the board and assures that:
  - the board does not overstep its limits;
  - the agendas for the board and executive committee meetings are developed in consultation with the head and sent out in advance of the meetings;
  - proper research is done on all issues, when necessary;
  - all issues are considered in a deliberative process; and
  - ample time is allocated for discussion.
- The chair usually leads the process for evaluating the head.
- The chair makes sure that the annual board self-assessment and the evaluation of the chair take place.
- The chair consults regularly with the head to anticipate and strategize issues, concerns, and priorities.
- The chair is a ready and willing listener to the head's concerns as they emerge; he or she serves as a major adviser.
- The chair is a private confidante, adviser, and critic when necessary. The chair is the head's No. 1 public advocate.
- The chair participates in the process of trustee selection and assures that the head has an opportunity to participate also and to review potential candidates and officers.
- The chair assures that trustee orientation occurs.
- The chair organizes the board in the most effective way to conduct its business, including the work of the executive committee.
- The chair provides particular oversight and direction to the school finances and resource management.

- The chair needs to involve his or her successor in discussions to assure a smooth transition at the conclusion of the current chair's term. Bringing the new chair up to speed is critical to the health of the board and the school.

- The chair accepts the responsibility to be the disciplinarian of the board when necessary and is willing to help counsel unproductive, disruptive, and counterproductive trustees off the board.

- The chair is willing to put in the time it takes to do all of these things. For most NAIS member school chairs, this task averages four to five hours a week over the course of the school year. Because the chair's responsibilities do not take a vacation, the chair will probably have to devote time to these issues during the summer months as well.

RESPONSIBILITIES OF THE HEAD IN THE CHAIR-HEAD RELATIONSHIP

- As the executive in charge of implementing policy and meeting goals, the head is responsible for the school's daily operations.

- The head informs and advises the chair through regular formal reports and in a number of informal ways.

JOINT RESPONSIBILITIES

- Together the chair and head articulate the school's mission and vision.

- Together they share responsibility for planning and regularly reviewing and evaluating current plans.

- Together they, along with the treasurer, oversee resource allocation.

- Together they remain aware that sometimes there will be areas in which lines of responsibility blur and ensure that open communication will help determine when joint presence and decision-making are most appropriate.

- Together they present a united front on all positions to the board, the school, and the larger community.

Cyril Houle, an expert on board-CEO relations, has noted some other instructive differences in the two positions:

Comparing the Roles of the Board, the Board Chair, and the Chief Executive

The Board	The Chair	The Head
Is corporate; can act only as a group	Cannot officially act alone	Is an individual
Exists continuously even as its membership changes	Changes often in many schools	Is temporary in the life of the school
Is part-time	Is part-time	Is full-time
Has little or no staff	Has little or no staff	Has access to all staff
Holds ultimate responsibility (along with the chair)	Holds ultimate responsibility (along with the full board)	Holds limited, immediate responsibility
Typically is not an expert in education	Typically is not an expert in education	Typically is an expert in education
Volunteer	Volunteer	Salaried
Sees only parts of the whole	Needs to be able to see the big picture	Is intimately involved in everything

ACKNOWLEDGING THE IMPACT OF LEADERSHIP CHANGE AND TURNOVER

How do we assure that the transition from one board chair to the next is a smooth one?

In their efforts to minimize the effect of leadership change on the school's forward momentum, board chairs and committees on trustees should be especially alert to the need for long-range planning for leadership succession. Who is best qualified to be the next board chair? What are his or her other commitments? Is he or she available? Who is a good alternative? Who's after that? Who will chair the capital campaign? Who will chair the committee on trustees, and when?

Every time a new chair steps on board, a school faces a critical moment. Since the current trend is for chairs to remain in office an average of only two years, the chair often lacks sufficient time to get to know the job and all he or she needs to about the school. Many step down just as the learning curve begins to flatten out, leaving a new chair to start all over again. A head has to learn to dance with a new partner every time the chair changes.

Heads' average tenure is now 8.1 years, according to NAIS research in 2002. Although a number of heads may stay at one school for 15 or 20 years or even longer, many others — as much as a third of NAIS heads today — have moved on to a second or third headship. They carry a lot of cumulative experience, but from different schools. It is common for heads who have been in the same place for six or seven years to find that no trustees on the current board were there when the heads started. No one remembers why the heads were selected or what was the process for determining long-range goals or shared accomplishments. It is possible that no one even agrees with those goals anymore. Even with a good strategic plan in place, it is hard for leaders to move the school forward when so little continuity exists.

It is a sad fact that many heads' unplanned departures in recent years stem from unplanned leadership changes, especially at the board chair level, which in turn have too often led to the unplanned departure of the head. These departures are inevitably disruptive to the school as parents, teachers, and students, as well as graduates and the broader world beyond the school, hold their breath and wait to see what will happen next. Anxiety goes up. Enrollment, fund raising, and faculty, student, and parent morale may go down for a period.

In the previous edition of this handbook, a key paragraph noted:

> Because the head and chair are partners, the premature resignation of a head is usually a sad reflection on the performance of the board chair. They succeed or fail together. If chair and head differ too greatly in style to be able to work together, the chair should consider resigning.

There is no clearer way to make the point today.

Each independent school is different, and so are its leaders. What works for one school or pair of leaders may not be comfortable for others. But for the sake of all constituents, it is important that head and chair try to maintain a consistent pattern of shared leadership to avoid sending mixed signals.

THE IMPORTANCE OF COMMUNICATION

To help these key school leaders learn best practices, NAIS established Leadership through Partnership, an annual workshop for heads and chairs in which the team spends two days hearing from outside experts. In the course of the weekend, they get to know each other better, too.

Each year at that workshop, heads have the opportunity to meet in small peer groups while chairs do the same. To get troublesome issues out in the open, facilitators provide thought-provoking questions such as "What is your pet peeve about your partner?" Interestingly, the answers from each group remain constant from year to year — but they are not, as one might anticipate, directly complementary.

THE FIRST RULE: NO SURPRISES

> How much do I need to share?

Board chairs are frequently concerned that heads do not communicate enough. This is noteworthy because heads often worry that they inundate chairs with information. Some heads are more deliberate about withholding information, but in general such a policy is apt to lead to misunderstanding or even trouble. How much communication is desired, how often, by what means, and when and where to share it will vary from school to school. The important thing is for head and board chair to answer the questions together. (Boarding schools may well depend heavily on e-mails, faxes, and a weekly or biweekly phone call; day schools may need e-mails, faxes, and perhaps more phone calls and more face-to-face meetings.)

For both parties, the first rule of communication is this: *No surprises.* A chair should know about major disciplinary incidents; faculty morale (up? down? why?); a new teacher who is shaky but getting special mentoring help; staff dismissals; trustee children who are not accepted at any of their college choices or into your very own school. And, obviously, the head needs to immediately communicate serious matters — such as a breaking news story or a tragedy — to the chair and then to all trustees, if appropriate. By getting the bad news quickly and from the highest level, the board chair can help strategize the head's response as needed.

The need to know corresponds to the need to be well prepared. When in doubt, the head should pick up the phone and the chair should willingly accept the call. Most often, the message requires no action from the chair, but the chair needs the information to be able to field phone calls from others and allay fears and rumors. Information sharing can also help the chair understand the pattern of daily life for the head.

Of course, the head should also share good news. A chair should get the first call (after the donor and the campaign chair) to rejoice in the school's first million-dollar gift, to learn that the middle school has performed 1,000 hours of community service, to be told that a teacher has been selected for a Klingenstein fellowship. Indeed, the head should share good news with all trustees. In return, the chair should share positive comments from people inside and outside the school community.

DISCIPLINING TRUSTEES: A JOB FOR THE CHAIR

A common pet peeve about board chairs is a very specific one: "I have a chair who will not discipline a maverick trustee." This person could be a renegade who stirs up trouble by ordering the staff around or by communicating inappropriately with other members of the board and the community. Most often, it is a trustee with a particular agenda, someone unwilling to work within established parameters.

> Why is this my job as chair?

The trustee who behaves inappropriately can be very damaging to the school, particularly if allowed to continue unchecked. In extreme cases, the chair may have to ask for a resignation or even take steps to remove a reluctant trustee. Often, however, a candid conversation will change the trustee's tactics. This is a conversation the chair should initiate and hold, not the head.

Doing this is hard, of course. The chair may say, "How can I discipline volunteers? They give their time and their money." Or "I didn't agree to do this when I signed up to be chair. Let's just let him ride out his term." Or "Maybe we can give her part of what she wants."

But no. The chair must intervene to head off, or stop, the problem.

TEAMWORK METAPHORS FOR HEAD AND CHAIR

Students of governance have proposed many images to describe the relationship between head and chair. Many of these images derive from the world of sports, where teamwork is so important. Let's look at three metaphors, each of which has something to offer a head and chair whether they are embarking on a new relationship or continuing an existing one.

1. A THREE-LEGGED RACE

Tell me about teamwork between head and chair.

To perform well in this race, the partners must agree on the pace they will set, who will stride forward with which leg, and in which direction they will go. If they are not in agreement, one will fall and both will be set back.

2. TENNIS DOUBLES

The older metaphor of tennis singles — where the chair tackles all policy issues on one side of a clearly defined barrier as the head tackles all management issues on the other side — was inadequate. True, there are some clear lines between the role of the board and the chair, and between the role of the administration and the head. But the lines are never so clear that everything on one side is unquestionably the board's business and everything on the other is the head's.

Many decisions require the best possible joint thinking, strategy, and action. Sometimes circumstances necessitate shared action. As in doubles, on occasion one player may need to take several shots in a row at the baseline or the net, even crossing over briefly into the other partner's space before returning to his or her own.

In some cases, local culture or circumstance may dictate that a chair take the lead on certain decisions even though normally the head would handle them. Chair and head must agree to respect each other's basic responsibilities — but they must also agree to avoid letting formal structure override common sense in specific instances. As in tennis, the partners who after a time are willing to critique each other's games while reducing points of friction are the ones who learn from experience and become a winning team.

3. THE CATCHER-PITCHER RELATIONSHIP

Yogi Berra, the famous New York Yankee catcher, once noted in *The New York Times* that spectators often think a catcher plays a secondary role in a pitcher's performance. "Pitchers," he wrote in a tone some board chairs may find familiar, "think they know everything." Obviously, neither pitchers nor heads of school know everything, even if they are experts on most of what is happening. The catcher's role is to suggest strategies about what to do when and how. Just as a pitcher can shake off a catcher's suggestion to throw a certain way, so can a head choose to "call the pitches." However, the wise head takes in and responds to good counsel from a good board chair.

Berra also said that a further responsibility of the catcher is to know "which guys to yell at and which you have to just pet." Of course, we are not recommending that a board chair either yell at or coddle a head of school. However, there are times when the chair must take the lead in encouraging, or discouraging, a head from continuing on the present course. Like the pitcher, the head is usually most visible as the leader. But like the catcher, the chair can make the team more effective by serving as ongoing strategist and coach. Metaphorically speaking, the chair can occasionally walk out to the mound to calm a head who made two or three bad pitches in a row, or even schedule a longer talk off the field when there's a losing streak. How effectively the catcher does this can help determine whether the team enjoys a winning game, or even a winning season. The same is true for the most effective board chairs.

As the board chair, you accept the role of coach, confidante, strategist, friendly critic, and No. 1 supporter of the head.

THE CHAIR AS OFFICIAL NURTURER OF THE HEAD

In addition to fulfilling the official responsibility to share information with a head, the chair must also be a major sustainer of a head's health and morale, even when the head has a supportive circle of family and friends. There are many ways to do this. The chair could provide a pair of tickets to the symphony, offer a beach house for the weekend, or suggest (or insist) that the head stay out of the office for two weeks at a time over the winter and spring breaks and for a full month in the summer.

> The head knows I care. Why do I have to say so?

Board chairs should also be aware that heads have lives outside of school and that at certain times family issues may take precedence over school issues. It is vital to recognize the need to have a support network for the head, who people too often assume should be willing to give 100 percent to the school. This need for support is a real one for the head, and acknowledging it comes with the territory for a board chair who plays a nurturing role.

THE CHAIR AS COMMUNICATOR OF A SERIOUS MESSAGE

How do we handle bad news?

From time to time, the board chair may have to share with the head bad news that is substantive and significant. It may be about something the head has done or not done, or something that has not been well received by some person or part of the school community. If the news is important, the chair should share it with the head as soon as possible — not wait for an annual evaluation.

This is not the kind of conversation to hold on the run or in a phone call. It deserves time and space of its own. The head needs a chance to reply immediately and perhaps more formally several days later, maybe after uncovering more information to help distinguish between fact and rumor. The perceived errors may be ones of omission or of commission.

After sharing the concern and hearing the head's response, the chair and head should strategize together to make sure they have a plan to resolve the present issue and minimize the chance of a recurrence. In most cases, the problem can be resolved and, with the chair's visible support, the relationship and the school can continue to move forward.

In rarer situations, a series of such conversations indicate to the head that the entire board believes it is time for the school to seek a new head for the year after next. In that final year, it is the special job of the board chair to ensure that the head can leave with a sense of dignity, clarity, and completion.

The essential elements in all such communication are trust, respect, candor, and a willingness to work to make the relationship better — and to help the school become more effective.

As board chair, you accept the responsibility to work with the head to resolve differences and problems throughout the head's tenure. As board chair, you understand the importance of clear, mutually established goals to the head's annual evaluation, to the board's evaluation, and to your own. As board chair, you understand that in accepting the leadership of the board, you make a serious commitment of mind and heart to the school and the head. You will work hard with the head and share, and enjoy, the challenge.

CASE STUDY

NEW HEAD, NEW METHODS

Thomas Stephens leaves a successful headship after eight years in a K-8 country day school and takes a new position as head of a K-12 day school in another state. His experiences as a skillful leader in his previous school and as a trustee of his state association of independent schools were clear factors in his appointment. He is nationally known for his close work with his several board chairs in implementing new models for board organization, particularly in reducing and streamlining board committees and increasing the number of ad hoc task forces to create more meaningful work for the board.

At the new school, Thomas and the board chair start the process of moving in this direction with the new board. Together they create two task forces, one focusing on technology and another on diversity issues. At the same time, they suspend the previous practice of having each committee report at each board meeting.

In late winter, the board chair unexpectedly takes a new job in a new city, so the vice chair takes over. The new chair, an alumna of the Class of 1957, learned her trusteeship in the traditional model, where board committees parallel the internal organization of the school (education, buildings and grounds, finance, etc.). That is the model she is comfortable with. She believes "if it ain't broke, don't fix it" and says she has heard from several trustees that they miss the opportunity to report on their committee work at each meeting. In her regular meeting with Thomas in early February, she tells him she has agreed to disband the task forces and return to the previous board organization. This is the first Thomas has heard of this turnaround.

What are the issues?
What should the head do?
What should the board do?
What should the chair do?

CASE STUDY

ADMINISTRATIVE EVALUATIONS: WHOSE BUSINESS ARE THEY, ANYWAY?

At the recommendation of an ISACS Visiting Team, this year Blackstone School has begun a formal evaluation program for all administrators, including the school head, Arthur Atwells. Arthur has met with the chair of the committee on trustees to review his own evaluation and, subsequently, with board chair Barbara Thayer to talk about the whole process.

During the course of the meeting he shares with Barbara the results of the evaluations of the division heads, deans, and department heads. A week later at the full board meeting, the topic of administrative evaluation is on the agenda. After a report on Arthur's evaluation, he is surprised to see Barbara preparing to hand around a stack of paper to the board.

"They're copies of the other administrators' reviews," Barbara explains. "I thought the board should have a look at them, especially since it's the first time we've gone through this."

"I really don't think that's appropriate," says Arthur. But several trustees, all of whom are parents in the school, are eager to see the material. As one says, "It's about time we got a chance to see how some of those people are really performing."

Arthur finally says, "I have to tell you that I consider this an inappropriate infringement on my responsibilities to hire and evaluate staff. I cannot accept this discussion and if it continues, I will have to leave the meeting and consider my options."

"Let's call a recess and discuss this," Barbara responds. The two head for Arthur's office, taking the stack of evaluations with them.

What are the issues?
What should Arthur and Barbara say to one another?
What do they say to the board?

This case study is by Richard Barbieri. For more governance case studies, go to www.nais.org, click on Resources and Statistics, and then on Governance Case Studies.

RESOURCES

Dietel, William M. and Linda R. Dietel. *The Board Chair Handbook.* Washington, DC: BoardSource,* 2001.

Gale, Robert L. *Leadership Roles in Nonprofit Governance.* Washington, DC: BoardSource,* 2003.

Hirzy, Ellen Cochrane. *The Chair's Role in Leading the Nonprofit Board.* Washington, DC: BoardSource,* 1998.

*Formerly the National Center for Nonprofit Boards

Houle, Cyril O. *Governing Boards: Their Nature and Nurture.* San Francisco, CA: Jossey-Bass, 1997.

Independent School Chairpersons Association, an organization for current and past board chairs: *www.iscachairs.org.*

CHAPTER 9

RELATING TO MAJOR CONSTITUENCIES OR STAKEHOLDERS

A S A TRUSTEE, you are a guardian of the school's human, financial, and physical resources, working to assure that they are sufficient to accomplish the school's goals and plans and are well managed. Your fellow trustees, the head, administrators, faculty, parents, students, graduates, funders, and friends are all major stakeholders of the school. You celebrate the diversity of the school's supporters and the diversity within groups of supporters.

A MULTIPLICITY OF RELATIONSHIPS

You interact with all of these stakeholders in formal, planned ways — such as at meetings and events — and in informal ways — such as in the parking lot or when walking across campus. Each relationship is different. Each brings its own set of rewards and potential problems. But if the school is fulfilling its mission with vision and energy, the school's constituents will all be bound together by this mission.

As a trustee, you need to be clear about how to manage both formal and informal contacts because a lack of clarity can lead to negative situations. With faculty, administrators, and other staff, you are the ultimate "boss"; after all, as a board member, you hire and evaluate the head, who in turn is the school's CEO and staff leader. You may be a parent or a graduate, yet you are part of the board whose decisions your friends may not like. With students, you may be seen as the mother or father of a friend or you may be off their radar screen altogether. If students do know about trustees and their role, you may be seen as just one more authority figure, making decisions that affect their lives for good or ill. With funders and friends from the community, you may share a great deal, such as living in the same neighborhood or working in the same building, or you may have barely or never met them. As a trustee, you must keep them in mind as you make decisions because the school's success may depend on their generosity with money, time, and expertise. However, you never let funders drive your decisions.

If you think your board member role can complicate your school relationships, you are right!

The trustee/head relationship is the most critical of all because it shapes the board's view of its interactions with administrators and faculty members. The head is the "gatekeeper" of the interaction between the trustees and the staff. She or he works with administrators and the chair to establish the parameters of the relationships and then shares the "rules" with all involved, trustees and staff alike. Board and staff can certainly meet and enjoy each other's company. However, they need to have a clear understanding of the communication chain and of the head's role as the point person for administrators and teachers, just as the chair is the point person for the board.

INTERACTING WITH ADMINISTRATORS AND FACULTY

Although not every school is able to afford a full complement of administrators, this discussion presupposes that there are paid professionals for most major functions. An important principle to remember: The trustees, head, and administrators exist to enable the faculty to fulfill the school's mission of providing an excellent education to its students.

FORMAL OPPORTUNITIES TO INTERACT

Most trustees work with administrators and faculty members while serving on committees or task forces. The individuals with whom board members interact most tend to be business managers, development directors, admission directors, academic division heads or deans, and teachers with special skills or an interest in serving on committees. Administrators often attend board meetings at least for part of the time and may give updates on activities they supervise.

INFORMAL OPPORTUNITIES TO INTERACT

Social and sporting events are among the places where trustees meet administrators and teachers most frequently. Day school trustees, especially those who are parents, run into staff members all the time around the school. Boarding school trustees have fewer opportunities to interact with teachers and administrators, but many such schools schedule social gatherings when trustees are on campus for their meetings.

REWARDS

Administrators and faculty members bring special expertise to planning and policy development. Because they are grounded in the school's day-to-day work, they can offer advice that serves as a valuable reality check on the board's deliberations. At the same time, they can visualize and articulate an exciting future for the school. They are colleagues of trustees as they all plan for and support the school and its students.

POTENTIAL PROBLEMS

Sometimes individual trustees and administrators or faculty forge alliances to circumvent the head, the board chair, and established procedures. Usually this happens over a grievance or a desire to further a personal agenda. As a trustee, do

> I never could stand Johnny's third-grade teacher, and he's still here!

not get drawn into a subversion of policies or procedures or an end-run around the head or chair. If you are not sure if policies or procedures (such as a grievance structure or communications plan) are already in place, find out. If they do not exist, work with the trustees, the head, or both to develop them and, where appropriate, bring them to the board for approval. Tell the head or chair any time teachers or administrators approach you to circumvent the established rules. The head should counsel her or his staff to do the same if a trustee contacts them improperly.

Faculty members sometimes have special relationships with trustees who are current or past parents because they have taught or are teaching the trustees' children. Over the course of a year, children and their teachers can have very positive or very negative interactions — or both. This experience can color the parents' relationship with the teachers and then carry over to board members' attitudes about individual teachers and the faculty as a whole. When advocating for their children with administrators or teachers, parent-trustees need to take off their trustee hat. Of course, it is hard for faculty to view trustee-parents without that hat. But board members need to focus on the well-being of the total staff and work collegially with individual members of their committees or task forces. Never use your position as a trustee to put added pressure on a faculty member or to gain unfair advantage for your child. In fact, good trustees often bend over backwards the other way, which may mean having their spouse or other family members interact most closely with their children's teachers. Clearly, this is a balancing act. As a parent, you should be an advocate for your children, but as a trustee you must not bring your personal concerns about an individual teacher to the board table.

A small percentage of boards have faculty members serving as ex-officio trustees, some with a vote and others without a vote. (Remember that ex-officio members have a vote unless the bylaws state that they serve "ex-officio, without a vote.") NAIS does not endorse this practice, as it can set up a troublesome dynamic. The heads are the "boss" of the faculty, yet faculty members serving on the board become the "boss" of the head. It can also be difficult for boards to have candid discussions about increasing the salary pool, the faculty workload, and so on when faculty members are present.

INTERACTING WITH PARENTS

You want me to tell the head that?

One of the most sensitive relationships for trustees is that with parents, especially when the trustee is also a parent of a child in the school.

FORMAL OPPORTUNITIES TO INTERACT

Board committee meetings frequently bring parents and trustees together. Non-trustee parents often serve on board committees, especially the development, buildings and grounds, and finance committees. Development and fund-raising activities also mix trustees, parents, and graduates together, whether the projects are annual and capital campaigns or special events. Schools may have policies that non-trustee parents may not serve on certain committees that deal with sensitive matters, especially the committee on trustees.

The parents association (also known as the parents' organization, the parents'/teachers' association, and the parents/teachers organization) welcomes parents and their children to the school, plans and implements parent nights and other parent forums, and raises funds in concert with the school's development plan. The chair of the association, or another representative, may serve on the board of trustees as an ex-officio member. But NAIS does not support such a practice for two reasons. First, most boards already have parents serving as term trustees and do not need to have an additional parent serving as a designated representative of the parent body. Second, term trustees do not represent any individual constituency because they are charged to be stewards for the school as a whole. Parent representatives, however, often believe that they should be stewards for current parents

It is very important for the board of trustees to keep the association leadership informed of the board's major decisions so that parent leaders can be prepared for questions from the parent body. If there is no formal personal liaison on the board, a system for informing association leaders should be established.

INFORMAL OPPORTUNITIES TO INTERACT

Day school board members have incredible opportunities to be with parents on and off school grounds — at parking lots, parties, athletic events, grocery stores, fund raisers, etc. Boarding schools may have the same opportunities if they also have a large number of day students. Otherwise, boarding-school trustees interact infrequently with the parent body and, when they do, most often it is at planned events.

Respecting parents

Parents take several major steps in support of the school's mission. They entrust their child to the school for her or his education. They expend a considerable amount of their financial assets to pay the tuition. They care deeply about the success of the school because its success benefits their child. Even though most of today's parents work outside the home, they volunteer in great numbers for almost every aspect of the school, and often they are generous donors to the annual and capital campaigns. Parents expect and deserve great consideration in board deliberations.

We couldn't do anything major without the support of the parents!

POTENTIAL PROBLEMS

Parents are very close to the school's program. They are consumers of what the school offers, and as such they question and question and question. This is not bad in and of itself, but it does become a problem when parents substitute their opinions for those of the experts hired to educate their children: the teachers. Many heads can tell stories of parents who constantly complain and then, when it is suggested that they might be happier at another school, become outraged. Parent-trustees who continually base their governance decisions on their personal experiences with their own children should be counseled off the board by the chair.

Trustees must not allow themselves to be drawn into the problems of families whose children attend their school. The trustees need to listen politely, tell the parents that trustees do not have any authority over their situation, ask them to talk to the appropriate administrator or the head, and then tell the head immediately about the conversation.

INTERACTING WITH FORMER STUDENTS

> What do you mean the school is going to change the color of the shutters?

A school's graduates can play critical roles on campus. Found among parents, funders, and trustees, they are living examples of the education the school provides.

FORMAL OPPORTUNITIES TO INTERACT

Graduates serve as trustees and are often involved in fund development activities in which they may play leadership roles. They host cultivation and fund-raising events for former students living in areas far from the school. Most schools have alumnae/i associations, which are the vehicles for graduates to express their opinions and to raise funds in coordination with the school's development plan. Often, the chair of the association or another representative serves ex-officio on the board of trustees and, in that capacity, the association chair or representative can bring graduates' issues to the attention of the board and board decisions back to the association. Increasingly, elementary schools are forming alumnae/i associations to encourage their graduates to provide the financial and other support they have traditionally given to their secondary schools and colleges.

INFORMAL OPPORTUNITIES TO INTERACT

Day schools have more of their graduates in the neighborhood than boarding schools do. However, in today's mobile society, day school graduates live all over the country. Trustees can meet them anywhere and everywhere, just as they do parents. It is an added joy for schools to have a good number of alumnae/i parents; entrusting one's own children to a school is the ultimate endorsement.

REWARDS

One hopes that graduates, wherever they find themselves, will be the best advertisement for the school. If the school keeps them well informed, former students can be enthusiastic and productive fund raisers since they are already deeply committed. Often they demonstrate this attachment when they help other graduates and current students with career planning and job hunting. Former students can be among the school's most valuable volunteers no matter where they live.

POTENTIAL PROBLEMS

Graduates who are disaffected and vocal can be very damaging to a school's reputation. Whether the problem is a distrust of current practices or unhappiness with their own student experiences, they can cause parents to question enrolling their children. When serving on the board of trustees or its committees, some former students have trouble with the ways the school has changed and thus balk at needed innovations; they perceive themselves as the keepers of tradition. Graduates such as these see the school as "their" school, not as their school and the school for current and future students. This is not to say that traditions are bad; they are very important for facilitating community building and a sense of connectedness to the past. Most current students are curious about the history of their school, especially the students who preceded them. But tradition should not be a barrier to the future. Rather, it should unify and be an opportunity for celebration.

INTERACTING WITH CURRENT STUDENTS

So that's why we're here!

The students are the reason for the school's existence — the reason for trustees, heads, faculty, and staff. They are why funds are raised, buildings are painted, plans are promulgated, committees meet, and on and on.

FORMAL OPPORTUNITIES TO INTERACT

To encourage students and trustees to mingle, some boards include students on committees or task forces and hold dinners with student leaders or even the whole student body. Schools hope that trustees will attend sporting events, plays, art exhibits, and debates to demonstrate support for the students and see them in action. Although this kind of contact can be difficult at boarding schools, many encourage it by scheduling student events when trustees have weekend meetings on campus.

INFORMAL OPPORTUNITIES TO INTERACT

These are more difficult to bring about because students are busy in school — or at least they should be! However, trustees can have conversations with students when they attend campus events. Today's students are not shy about sharing their opinions, concerns, and joys. Of course, parent-trustees have myriad occasions to interact with students, including driving carpools and sitting around the kitchen table.

REWARDS

Students bring immediacy to issues because they are such an important part of the educational equation. Just as faculty and parents have opinions about how the school should implement its program, so do students. Trustees need to value students' ideas and check in through appropriate ways to assess how students feel about their school. Of course, they are children, but often children's views can be just as on target as adults'. Age alone does not guarantee wisdom.

POTENTIAL PROBLEMS

Trustees need to avoid becoming involved with a particular student's problem, whether it concerns academics or behavior. Students are not perfect; they do get into trouble — even model students. Fortunately, they usually do not ask their parents (or another adult connected with the school) to intervene on their behalf. The problems arise when a concerned parent or friend's parent is a trustee who cannot separate the parent role from that of trustee.

INTERACTING WITH FUNDERS AND FRIENDS

Funders and friends from beyond the immediate school community are valuable not only for their financial contributions but also for their connections and advice. Corporate foundations seldom fund independent schools except by matching employee gifts. However, private independent and family foundations can be very generous benefactors. Other friends of the school may be educators from all areas and levels of education, community leaders, neighbors of the school, vendors, and so on. They feel connected to the school, but not as directly as the constituents mentioned above do.

FORMAL OPPORTUNITIES TO INTERACT

Schools may invite funders to events honoring their gifts, to educational programs, for scheduled visits to see what their gifts have enabled, and so on. Members of the community at large should be welcome to attend educational programs, visual and performing art shows, and the like whenever it is appropriate and does not take away from the primacy of the students, their program, and their needs. This is "friend raising" at its broadest and best.

INFORMAL OPPORTUNITIES TO INTERACT

As already noted, you may not always know that you are in the presence of funders and friends. As a trustee, you need to be prepared to advocate for the school at any moment and in any place you find yourself.

REWARDS

"Outsiders" — funders and friends alike — can bring new perspectives, financial support, and wisdom to the school. They can expand the school's reach to more diverse populations and become allies in promoting the school to their own friends.

POTENTIAL PROBLEMS

Funders sometimes offer resources with conditions. By accepting gifts with strings attached, over time the school may or may not be solvent, but it will have lost its integrity and its board members will have abdicated their moral trusteeship.

INTERACTING WITH NEIGHBORS

As student populations expand and their need for more buildings and more land grows, schools can find themselves in disputes with their community. Zoning issues, architectural styles, parking, and use of buildings by non-school groups on weekends are only a few of the issues that can pit schools against the neighbors. This antagonism can lead to all types of actions — from yard signs proclaiming "Stop School X" to litigation. Trustees, along with the head and other administrators, can play an important role in community relations, whether by meeting with neighborhood associations or by speaking to zoning boards. Schools that have positive relationships with their neighbors work very hard at them. They keep neighbors informed of pending changes before they actually take place and, when possible, offer their facilities to neighbors for meetings, sporting activities, and the like. They also invite them to plays, concerts, art exhibits, and athletic events.

WORKING WITH EDUCATIONAL ASSOCIATIONS

Many schools are involved with local, state, regional, and national independent school associations as well as ones for specific segments of the independent school community, such as boarding schools, girls' schools, and religiously affiliated schools. Trustees need to be aware of and support these relationships by encouraging administrators and faculty members to participate in these organizations. Trustees themselves can be valuable board members for these associations.

Independent schools can also have very positive, rather than competitive, relationships with public school systems and individual public schools. Such partnerships frequently strengthen both public and private institutions, which have much to give to and learn from each other.

As a trustee, you work to keep the diverse stakeholders of the school connected to each other and to keep their interests and needs in your thoughts during board deliberations. You do this even as you make decisions in the best interests of the school as a whole. You relish the diversity of perspectives, talents, and backgrounds, especially nurturing the strengths and potential of each and every student. You are the guardian of their well-being and that of generations of students to come. You hold the school's future in your hands.

CASE STUDY

CHANGING TIMES, CHANGING DEMANDS

Pippin School, in the California farming town of Appleborough, has for 65 years served as the region's only independent school option. A K–8 school, it accepts nearly all applicants except those with significant learning differences. Its families reflect a range of socioeconomic backgrounds, from small-town business owners to professionals to working farm families. Graduates attend local public schools for the most part, though a few venture to more distant independent high schools.

In recent years, due to suburbanization and improved highways, Appleborough has become something of a bedroom community for Big Orchard 60 miles away. This trend has brought many more prosperous families to the old farms and ranches. Over the past three or four years, new parents, including some recently appointed to the board, have pointed with alarm to the fact

that school test scores consistently fall below the national independent school averages. Demands for "academic excellence" and greater challenges have come from parents whose children score high or who hope their children will attend the most selective colleges.

At the traditional open board meetings in June, several parents accuse the board of shirking its responsibility to oversee the educational program and demand that the school adopt higher academic standards for the coming year. Two board members announce their complete agreement with these parents. The meeting ends in a mood of distress and unhappiness.

What are the issues?
What should the board do?
What should the chair of the board do?
What should the head do?

RESOURCES

Ellis, Susan J. *The Board's Role in Maximizing Volunteer Resources.* Washington, DC: BoardSource,* 1999.

E-volunteerism: The Electronic Journal of the Volunteer Community. Online newsletter.

The Head's Letter. Portsmouth, RI: Educational Directions, Inc. Newsletter published nine times yearly.

*Formerly the National Center for Nonprofit Boards

"Parents and Independent Schools." Glen Burnie, MD: Association of Independent Maryland Schools.

The Trustee's Letter. Portsmouth, RI: Educational Directions, Inc. Newsletter published fives times yearly.

CHAPTER 10

ORGANIZING AN EFFECTIVE BOARD

AS A TRUSTEE, you are part of a diverse and complicated school community. You work to assure that the board is effective and focused on its work of fulfilling the mission and bettering the well-being of its community. You do not "run" the school; you govern through planning, monitoring, and evaluating. You add value to the board's life and to the life of the school.

HOW NONPROFIT AND FOR-PROFIT BOARDS COMPARE

An independent school is a business — in the business of education. Like a for-profit corporation, a school needs a positive financial balance at the end of the fiscal year and achieves it by prudently managing all of its resources. Having either a budget deficit or a large surplus indicates poor planning or a failure to adjust properly during the year.

Also like a for-profit, schools have missions, governing boards, board chairs, meetings, budgets, etc. Boards in both sectors set the mission, oversee the accomplishment of goals, and hire the CEO. However, the models differ in important ways, as the following table shows.

GOVERNANCE OF FOR-PROFITS VS. INDEPENDENT SCHOOLS

	For-Profit Businesses	Independent Schools
Mission	To grow sales of goods and services	To educate students
Organizational structure	Hierarchical	Oriented toward community and collegiality
Success measurement	Determined by bottom-line financial performance	Determined by multiple soft and hard outcomes, including financial performance
Board size	Small, including many insider salaried officers	Large, without salaried staff, except that many schools have the head serve on the board and a few schools have a faculty member
Board membership	• Compensated • Serves for the long term • Chosen for skills and experience tied to specific business needs	• Expected to give and get funds • Serves for limited terms • Drawn from diverse constituencies, usually for broad skills and experiences
Board leadership	CEO is in charge of the board and the business	CEO (head) may or may not be on the board but, even when on the board, is not its leader
Board organization	Nominating committee is not active	Committee on trustees is the most important committee

BOARDS' ORGANIZATIONAL STRUCTURES

This chapter will describe the organizational and meeting structures that reflect current thinking on how boards can be most effective in accomplishing their work. The committees that are not part of this "model" will be described at the end of this chapter. The word "model" appears in quotation marks because the structures described here are just suggestions; the most effective boards develop their own structures annually around the school's own strategic priorities. Board and staff should work together to determine the critical issues facing the school and to forward the agenda. Both trustees and the head need to understand what truly matters to the school's stakeholders, and this means that trustees need to have in-depth interaction with the school's constituencies. Trustees also need to enlist the advice of experts, some of whom may be on the board and others who may not be. After learning what really matters, the board and head work collaboratively to develop and implement policy and then use predetermined measurements to monitor its effectiveness.

This style of interaction fuses the traditional lines of policy development with implementation. The board structure is issue-based, ad hoc, and flexible. There are fewer standing committees and more task forces. These task forces are charged with investigating strategic issues and bringing policy recommendations to the board and administration. Agendas change from meeting to meeting, and the board becomes energized because it is clear that every trustee's input is valued and the board's collective wisdom makes a difference to the school. Thus an effective board is a "constellation," not a collection of "stars," as stated by author Barbara E. Taylor and other board experts.

BOARDS' STANDING COMMITTEES

Even boards that spend most of their time on strategic issues need a few standing committees, including the following.

COMMITTEE ON TRUSTEES

This committee coordinates the identification, cultivation, recruitment, and orientation of new trustees; renominates sitting trustees; nominates officers; facilitates board self-assessment; identifies the board's needs for education and training and designs vehicles to meet those needs; and organizes the recognition of individual trustees. At some schools, the committee nominates members of the committee on trustees for election by the board. At other schools, members of the committee are appointed in the same manner as all committees are. All nominations are sent to the board for its approval. (See Chapter 6 for more information.)

FINANCE (ASSET OVERSIGHT/RESOURCES) COMMITTEE

This committee is involved with the following functions:

- **Finances.** In concert with staff, the committee develops the long-range financial plan and yearly operational budget, including setting tuition levels for board approval; monitors the implementation of the budget; makes periodic reports to the board on the school's financial status; and educates the board on nonprofit financial reporting and trends affecting the school's finances. (For more information on the board's role in assuring the school's financial well-being, see Chapter 5.) This committee's members can include outside experts on finances and financial planning.

- **Investments.** The committee develops and recommends to the board for its approval policies that delineate how the school will invest its endowment and what amount of return on investment the school will use in its yearly operating budget; monitors the investment portfolio's return, including setting investment objectives and meeting with the professional adviser; and periodically reports to the board on the endowment's performance. A subcommittee of the finance committee, rather than the total committee, can oversee investments. Some finance or investment subcommittees actually manage endowment funds, but this practice is not recommended because of the objective expertise and time necessary to do a truly effective job. (See Chapter 5.)

- **Building and grounds (property).** The committee develops the master plan for the school's buildings and grounds with the staff and outside consultants (if the school employs consultants) for board approval; monitors implementation of the plan; reports to the board periodically on major plant and campus issues; and keeps the finance committee informed of buildings and grounds needs. Sometimes the committee provides board oversight of major building projects, but it does not act as the project manager. (A special board task force can be formed to oversee a major project for its duration.) The committee does not get involved in day-to-day operations, such as roof leaks, playing-field maintenance, carpet selection, etc., but it should be especially attentive to the deferred maintenance needs of the plant. Among its members can be parents, others with expertise in construction and allied fields, and students. It can be a discrete subcommittee of the larger finance committee.

AUDIT COMMITTEE

This committee should be independent of the finance committee because part of the audit function may include evaluating the finance committee's oversight of the school's resources. The audit committee recommends the independent auditor for board approval; works with the auditor to establish the scope of the audit; reviews the recommendations for improving internal controls as noted in the auditor's management letter; recommends approval of the annual audit to the board; and monitors the implementation of the recommendations of the management letter. This is the committee that has oversight over the school's major business and operational risks to assure the board that the risks are being identified and managed appropriately. (See Chapter 5.)

DEVELOPMENT (ADVANCEMENT) COMMITTEE

This committee coordinates the school's fund-raising activities; advises the board on the financial goals of the annual campaign, and on any capital or endowment campaign; reviews the case statement for all fund-raising appeals; facilitates including all trustees and other volunteers in fund- and friend-raising activities; and raises funds. This committee should not be viewed as the only group that brings in financial resources. All trustees should be involved in fund development. (See Chapter 5's Sample Materials for ways in which board members can get involved.) In addition, parents and graduates should be involved in ways that are appropriate for them. Of course, everyone on the committee should give gifts themselves before soliciting funds from others. (See Chapter 5 for more information on the board's role in assuring the financial strength of the school.)

EXECUTIVE COMMITTEE

This committee coordinates, with the board chair, the work of the board; serves as a sounding board for the head; acts in place of the board between board meetings in the manner prescribed by the bylaws and as expressly delegated by the board; and reports any actions to the board in a timely fashion. However, this is not a super-board. It does not make policy. If the executive committee takes over the board's role, the board will either become passive and uninvolved, or angry. Neither reaction leads to effective governance.

Schools with a large number of trustees find the executive committee an essential tool for organizing the board's work. Boarding schools may also use executive committees as a means to keep a core of board members involved. Because the full board tends to meet only three to four times a year and many trustees live far from the boarding school, these committee members need to be especially vigilant in assuring that the board, not the executive committee, is the governing body of the school.

The bylaws usually state who should serve on the executive committee. Most often, it is the officers and chairs of the standing committees and strategic task forces. Some executive committees have members at large, appointed by the chair.

Note: The functions of the committees that are not included in this list but exist on some boards become subsumed in the work of the task forces or the executive committee on an as-needed basis. They include admissions and marketing, advice to the head, education, financial aid, personnel, strategic planning, and student life. (See more about these committees on page 183.)

COMMITTEE AND TASK FORCE ASSIGNMENTS

How did I end up on this committee?

A school's bylaws normally give the board chair the authority to appoint committee or task force chairs. Once the chairs are in place, committee membership is then generally selected in one of two ways:

- The board chair appoints committee members, usually in consultation with the committee chairs and head of school.
- The committee chairs choose the members of their committees, usually in consultation with the board chair and head of school.

Many schools ask their trustees to indicate their committee/task force preferences in ranked order of interest. The committee on trustees, acting in its board development role, may recommend specific trustee assignments to the board chair for members who are being groomed for leadership positions. The idea is to move trustees beyond their areas of expertise to a broader knowledge of the work of the entire board. This experience will make them better board leaders when their time comes.

BOARD SIZE

One of the governance questions NAIS hears most often is, "What should the size of the board be?" There is no perfect size. According to a 2001 NAIS leadership study, the average number of trustees on NAIS member schools' boards is 22, but that really is not a guide to the "right" number for your

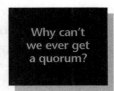

What is the perfect number of trustees?

school. The ideal is the smallest number of trustees that allows your board to be effective. Many factors influence board size, including the size of the school, whether it is a day or boarding school, and the range of grades. However, the key factor in board size is the board's organizational structure. If there is a multiplicity of committees or task forces, even with a large number of non-trustee participants, the board will need to be larger than one that has fewer committees and focuses on strategic issues through the use of task forces. A board is too large when (1) the chair has to spend an inordinate amount of time managing the work of the board rather than leading the board and (2) when staff members must devote their scarce time to generating mounds of paper, assisting at a multitude of meetings, etc.

BOARD MEETINGS

SUCCESSFUL BOARD MEETINGS

No matter how a board is organized, its meetings need to focus on issues that further the school's mission and vision; evaluate current policies; and assess the performance of the school, the head, and the board itself. Meetings should not end up as events where intelligent, talented, and thoughtful people gather to approve minutes and listen to reports that just as easily could have been mailed.

Why can't we ever get a quorum?

What are the characteristics of successful board meetings? They should:
- inform, educate, and inspire trustees;
- make good use of the assembled expertise to benefit the school;
- involve examining strategic directions through in-depth discussion;
- identify and resolve conflict; and
- reach conclusions, whether by a formal vote or consensus.

The board chair, in consultation with the head, should develop the board agendas. Once the meeting begins, the agenda belongs to the board as a whole; the chair merely facilitates discussion. Fifty percent of the meeting time should be devoted to education, training, and strategic-issue discussion. Board development is important for all trustees, not just new ones. It seems only appropriate for trustees of educational institutions to value education for themselves. Some large boards break into smaller groups for this type of discussion and, upon reconvening, summarize their group's conversation and conclusions for the total board. Using different discussion methods and educational styles can add energy to board meetings. (See the Sample Materials section of this chapter for an agenda example.)

Boards do need reports to accomplish their business, but there are ways to get the information to the board without tying up the meetings and wasting valuable time:

- Mail minutes and reports out in advance.
- Since reports are mailed, only allow questions on the reports or brief updates on critical activities or developments.
- Discuss reports that require action and then act on the report's recommendations.
- Do not "accept" or "approve" a report. Those two words mean the same thing, and when board members make such a motion, they are saying they agree with every word in the report and certify its accuracy. This is particularly problematic with financial reports. Only after the annual independent audit can trustees be assured that the figures are accurate. Then they can approve the audit report.

Part of your responsibility as a trustee is to be sure you have the information you need to make reasoned decisions. Is the information clear? Are there too many facts and figures, or too few? Is it on target, or are you missing critical items? Boards that meet three or four times a year have special information needs that require developing a means of effective communication between meetings. Here are other hints for effective board meetings.

- Remember that a skilled board chair makes all the difference. If the board chair is not experienced in running meetings or lacks knowledge of parliamentary procedure, find a mentor, or "tutor," to help train the chair. The committee on trustees can require this step of potential chairs and should find resources to meet this need.
- Group action items together and keep them separate from discussion items. This helps the board get through the necessary matters efficiently and leaves ample time for issue discussion — the part of the meeting that trustees value most.
- Make certain that the board expects and establishes proper trustee

behavior at meetings. This includes candor, respect, individual ownership of one's opinions, active participation in discussions, confidentiality, etc.

- Meet trustees' needs for a basic knowledge of parliamentary procedure. Parliamentary procedure protects the rights of the minority to be heard and the majority to make decisions. (See the simple guide to parliamentary procedure at the end of this chapter.)
- Establish an annual plan that includes a calendar of the board's work and a process to bring committee recommendations to the board in a timely manner.
- Start and end your meetings on time. Schedule the amount of time necessary to accomplish the agenda — no more, no less.
- Use a timed agenda if the board has difficulty bringing closure to discussions. Times can be changed during the meeting by consent or by a formal board vote.
- Make sure that the minutes work for the board. The following are ways to improve minutes.
  - Do not record debate unless a general sense of the issues will explain the actions taken at the meeting or will inform future actions.
  - Capitalize, boldface, or underline motions so that they're easy to find within the body of the minutes. Do likewise with "motion carried" or "motion defeated."
  - Attach full reports to the official minutes and send any reports given out at the meeting to those who were absent.
  - Give motions in writing to the secretary to assure accuracy.
  - Have a cover page summary listing all the major actions of the meeting.
  - Put the notice about the next meeting at the top of the summary page or on the first page of the minutes.
  - Have the secretary put his or her name and title at the end of the minutes. According to parliamentary procedure, the secretary should never use the words "respectfully submitted." If the secretary is not respectful, then he or she should not be the secretary! Once the board has approved the minutes, the secretary should sign the official copy.
  - Some boards have staff actually take the minutes. Then the secretary, and sometimes the chair, reviews them before they are sent to the board. Even in this case, the board secretary would sign the official copy.

BOARD MEETING FREQUENCY AND LENGTH

We meet every month for an hour and a half and still can't finish the agenda!

Two other frequently asked questions are, "How often should boards meet?" and "How long should the meetings last?" The answer to both is, "That depends." The number of meetings should be based on the type of school (boarding schools meet less frequently than most day schools) and on the organizational structure of the board (those with more committees often meet less frequently than those that do much of their work as a full board). The typical day school board meets in the evening over the course of nine to 10 months of the year. About one-third of all schools meet three to four times a year, with boarding schools at the lower end of the spectrum. The average number of meetings per year is about seven to eight.

Note: Boards that send their reports out in advance and spend most of their meeting time on issue discussion, education, and training tend to meet every other month. Committees and task forces meet in the months between the board meetings.

Board-meeting length also depends on the type of school. Most boarding school boards come together for one to two days and combine committee and board meetings during that time period. The actual amount of time that boarding school trustees spend in their meeting can be longer than day schools, where board meetings range from one to four hours. The goal of a board meeting is not to finish as quickly as possible but to have sufficient time for deliberations, education, and training.

Committee meetings should be based on the same principles as board meetings. However, these meetings tend to be more informal, and committee actions can be recorded in the form of notes rather than minutes. Formal motions should always be recorded. Remember, committees should schedule their meetings so that when their recommendations need board action, the board can receive the recommendations in a timely manner before the board meets.

BOARD MEETINGS: OPEN OR CLOSED?

What does the board do when a parent or group wants to attend a board meeting to advance an agenda?

In most circumstances, board meetings are closed to individuals other than the trustees and head. However, there are exceptions. The school's business manager and director of development may often be present as expert advisers. In addition, other administrators, faculty members, non-trustee committee members, students, and outside community members may be invited to attend a board meeting to share their expertise on specific issues before the board. Typically, though, these people are present at the meeting only during the time their expertise is needed. Outsiders who have not been privy to board discussions of the issues, or who are single-issue advocates, can distort the climate and direction of conversation.

That being said, keep these two points in mind. First, if you have questions about the impact of your state's Sunshine Laws on public access to your meetings or minutes, you should consult your school's legal counsel. Second, NAIS does support open-book management and encourages boards to highlight board and committee agendas, board actions, and minutes in periodic communications to constituents and on the school website. Although non-board members are seldom, if ever, invited to board meetings, they are often invited to committee or task force meetings. In fact, it is good practice to populate committees and task forces with opinion leaders from outside the board.

BOARD OFFICERS

The final ingredient in the recipe for excellent governance is high-caliber leaders of the leaders: the officers of the board. All trustees are leaders of the school and are equally responsible for it. However, officers agree to assume additional duties in order to facilitate board work. They are not elevated to some lofty state. They are the servants of the board. (For the important characteristics of all officers, see Chapter 6.)

Each school's bylaws should state the major responsibilities for each officer in a very brief form. Full job descriptions should be developed for each position and reviewed every few years. The following are meant to serve as the starting point for such descriptions.

The chair (or president), the chief volunteer officer. She or he
- Works in partnership with the head to achieve the school's mission and presents a united front to the world at large.
- Manages the board and coordinates its work in collaboration with the executive committee.
- Develops board and executive committee agendas in collaboration with the head.

- Presides at board and executive committee meetings.
- Appoints chairs of committees, with the approval of the executive committee, when required to do so by the bylaws.
- Serves ex officio on all committees and task forces but does not need to attend every meeting. Chooses to attend the critical meetings (such as those of the committee on trustees and finance) when critical issues are being discussed.
- Plays a leading, visible role in fund development activities, including asking board members for their financial contributions.
- Assumes major responsibility for evaluating the head.
- Represents the board at internal and external events.
- Acts as the chief cheerleader for the school and its students.

Vice chair (or vice president). On some boards there is more than one. The vice chair can:
- Preside over board and executive committee meetings in the absence of the chair.
- Represent the school at internal and external events in the absence of the chair.
- Assume other responsibilities as assigned by the chair, including chairing a committee or task force.
- Coordinate the work of the committees or task forces as one way to free up the chair to focus on leading the whole board, fund raising, and working with the head.

Note: Some schools have the officer position of chair-elect. This person usually has the same responsibilities as a vice chair, with the added expectation that she or he will become the chair when the current chair's term ends.

Secretary. This officer is responsible for board and executive meeting minutes. As noted above, some schools have staff take the actual minutes during the meeting. But the secretary of the board is ultimately responsible for the content. In the absence of the secretary at a meeting, the chair can appoint a secretary pro-tem. The secretary should examine previous minutes to see if there is any unfinished business and, if so, bring such business to the chair's attention for inclusion on the next meeting's agenda. In many jurisdictions, the secretary must sign legal documents in compliance with local statutes.

Treasurer. The treasurer interprets the organization's financial information to the board; brings up financial issues for board consideration; chairs the finance committee unless another trustee fulfills this function; facilitates the committee's development of policies and the budget; and leads its monitoring of budgeted income and expenses.

Note: Some boards have bylaws that give an inaccurate description of the treasurer's duties. Remember that the treasurer is not the school's chief financial officer, business manager, or even the bookkeeper.

ADDITIONAL COMMITTEES FOUND ON BOARDS

Some of the following committees may become advisory bodies to the administration and consist in part or in whole of non-trustees.

The **admissions/marketing committee** reviews admissions policies and standards, marketing literature, the master calendar for school promotion, and strategies for recruiting students and doing ongoing cultivation of their families. The committee can encourage and oversee communications plans and also oversee financial-aid policies if that charge is not part of a financial-aid committee (described below). The committee does not play any role in admitting students or awarding financial aid.

The **head's advisory committee**, whose members are selected by the head, counsels the head on her or his concerns with individuals or constituent groups. This committee can be of assistance when differences arise between the head and trustees, including the chair. The group usually consists of two to three members and does not include the chair. Although most boards do not have this committee, some schools use it during the new head's first year only to support her or his entry into the new community. It is often called the transition committee and may include special support for the head's family. Several major problems can arise if a head's advisory committee becomes the gatekeeper for trustee access to the head, is confused with the executive committee, or stands in the way of what should be a close relationship between the head and board chair.

The **education committee** concentrates on issues at the broadest level; develops and recommends to the board educational policies, such as the type of education offered at the school (college prep, arts, vocational, elementary, high school, etc.); assesses the overall school performance against the strategic plan; can play a major role when the school is in the accreditation process; and reports periodically to the board. This committee does not set the curriculum or evaluate teachers. Committee members can include school faculty, administrators, and outside educators. This committee is rapidly disappearing from the array of independent school board committees, no matter what the board structure is.

Note: Trustees who are members of the education committee often find such service frustrating, as the curriculum is the responsibility of the head and faculty and the committee's role is not clear. In fact, a number of boards have decided against having such a committee and instead handle major educational issues through the strategic planning process.

The financial-aid committee works with staff to develop policies concerning the eligibility and administration of aid; recommends policies to the board; and recommends, through the budget process, the percentage of the budget dedicated to financial aid. It does not decide who will get aid or how much aid will be given to a student.

The personnel committee works in cooperation with the head to develop broad personnel policies, such as benefits, salary ranges, and the requirements for faculty and staff evaluation. The committee recommends to the board, through the budget process, salary pool increases. However, it does not get involved in implementing the policies, such as setting individual salaries.

The strategic planning committee works in concert with the head, faculty members, and administrators to develop the strategic plan for board approval, including its mission statement, goals, and strategic issues. The committee can also monitor the plan's implementation. Often, the committee is limited in time, acting essentially as a task force, because the executive committee or other committees whose charge touches on specific sections of the plan monitor the implementation. The head is responsible for developing action plans unless the goal concerns governance issues. The committee can include non-trustee parents and outside experts. (See Chapter 6 for more information.)

The student life committee concerns itself with broad policy issues beyond academic areas, such as the breadth of extracurricular and sports programs and the building of community. The committee works with the head to develop and implement opportunities for trustees and students to interact. It does not plan specific student activities, such as which sports to offer. Students make excellent committee members, as their perspective can be very helpful.

As a trustee, you are a member of the leadership team that is the board. You work collegially with other trustees and the head to achieve the board's agenda. You serve on at least one committee or task force and accept assignments as best you can within your time constraints. Remember that if you agree to serve as a trustee, you not only need to make the school a priority in your financial giving, but it must also be a priority in your commitment of time. When asked, you embrace service as an officer, knowing that this is a special opportunity to contribute your talents to the school for which you are the guardian.

CASE STUDY

RESISTING SELF-EVALUATION

The board of the Thompson School has reviewed the school's most recent accreditation report and has noted with particular interest the comments of the visiting committee under the governance section. "We recommend," the visiting committee noted, "that the board of trustees consider creating a process of annual self-evaluation to complement its annual evaluation of the head of school." The chair brings this recommendation to the full board for discussion, but the first responses from the floor include comments such as, "How can we evaluate the work of volunteers? We — they — give much to the school, of time and money and other resources." "It would not be fair to evaluate them." "We might lose their interest and support."

The head and chair join in the conversation, noting that both national and local independent school organizations, as well as BoardSource, recommend that the board regularly evaluate itself and its own leadership, and evaluate the head. But as the meeting adjourns, with agreement that the topic will be revisited at the next meeting, it is obvious that the recommendation did not sit well with a significant portion of the board.

What are the issues?
What should the chair do?
What should the head do?

S A M P L E   M A T E R I A L S

SAMPLE BOARD MEETING AGENDA

I. Call to Order — A welcome from the chair, who also shares the objectives of the meeting and reviews the agenda.

II. Consent Agenda*** — A device to shorten meetings. The items on this agenda are passed by consent (without a vote, if there is no objection) or by formal vote. Single items can be taken off the agenda and considered separately, if even only one member wishes to do so. Typical items on this agenda are minutes, routine ratification, and board approval required by the bylaws, such as the approval of banking relations. As a matter of risk management, never put the treasurer's report in a consent agenda because the figures have not been audited and the board does not want to be held legally accountable for what could be inaccurate numbers.

III. Treasurer's Report *** — An opportunity for the treasurer to answer questions on financial reports or bring items for action.

IV. Head's Report *** — An opportunity for trustees to ask questions on the written report and for the head to share confidential items she or he did not want to put in writing. The head can also use this time to update trustees on broad educational issues and trends.

V. Committee/Task Force Reports *** — These begin with committees and task forces, which have action items, and then allow time for questions on other reports. Remember that committees and task forces do not need to be on every agenda if they have neither sent out a report nor proposed action items.

VI. Issues Discussion/In-Depth Board Education *** — This area of the agenda should get 50 percent of the board's meeting time unless a committee or task force has major business to bring for a board decision during the report section above. Task forces can use this time to solicit input from trustees on the strategic issue they are examining. This is the part of the agenda where the board can break into smaller groups or have interactive education or training.

VII. Old (Unfinished) Business — Items that have been postponed from or not finished at previous meetings.

VIII. New Business — An opportunity for any trustee to bring up items that have not been placed on the agenda. However, it is not good practice for board members to bring up major issues at this time because there likely would not be time for a thorough discussion. Besides, most board members, and certainly the chair and head, do not like surprises!

IX. Evaluation of the Meeting — Can be a two-minute quick appraisal. The board answers two questions: "What went well?" and "What did not?"

X. Adjournment

*** Materials sent to trustees in advance of the board meeting

S A M P L E   M A T E R I A L S

PARLIAMENTARY PROCEDURE AT A GLANCE

To do this	Say...
Adjourn the meeting*	"I move that we adjourn."
Recess the meeting	"I move that we recess until..."
Complain about room temp, etc.*	"Question of privilege."
Suspend further consideration of something*	"I move that the motion be laid on the table."
End debate	"I move the previous question."
Postpone consideration of something*	"I move to postpone this matter until..."
Have something studied further	"I move to refer the motion to the XXX committee."
Amend a motion	"I move that..."
Introduce business (a primary motion)	"I move that..."
Object to procedure or to a personal affront*	"Point of order."
Request information*	"Point of information."
Ask for a vote by actual count to verify a voice vote*	"I call for a division."
Object to consideration of some undiplomatic matter*	"I object to the consideration of the question."
Take up a matter previously tabled	"I move to take from the table."
Reconsider something already disposed of	"I move to reconsider."+
Consider something out of its scheduled order*	"I move we suspend the rules and consider..."
Vote on a ruling by the chair*	"I appeal from the decision of the chair."

* Not amendable

+ Motion can only be made by someone on the previously prevailing side.

May you interrupt the speaker?	May you be seconded?	Is the motion debatable?	What vote is required?
No	Yes	No	Majority
No	Yes	No	Majority
Yes	No	No	No vote
No	Yes	No	Majority
No	Yes	Yes	2/3 vote
No	Yes	Yes	Majority
No	Yes	Yes	Majority
No	Yes	Yes	Majority
No	Yes	Yes	Majority
Yes	No	No	Chair decides
Yes	No	No	No vote
No	No	No	No vote
Yes	No	No	No vote
No	Yes	No	Majority
Yes	Yes	Yes	Majority
No	Yes	Yes	2/3 vote
Yes	Yes	Yes	Majority

SAMPLE MATERIALS

A TRUSTEE SURVIVAL GUIDE

NAIS President Patrick F. Bassett, formerly president of the Independent Schools Association of the Central States, offers the following list of items each trustee should have. It comes from ISACS' *Trustee Handbook/Board Policies Book.*

1. School mission statement

2. Brief history of the school

3. Directories: trustee, faculty, parent/student

4. Board committees: structure, charges, and assignments

5. Calendars: for the school year and for board and committee meetings

6. Budget/audit

7. Endowment report

8. Strategic plan

9. NAIS's complete Principles of Good Practice

10. Bylaws

11. Admission catalog and application package

12. School placement profile

13. School statistics (enrollment, financial operations, annual giving, tuition, salaries, etc.)

14. Copy of NAIS's *Trustee Handbook*

15. Minutes from last year

16. Board policies: endowment, conflict of interest, nondiscrimination, harassment, financial aid, admission, staffing and personnel, board resolutions, etc.

17. Handbooks: employee and parent/student

18. Board orientation procedures and schedule

RESOURCES

Bobowick, Marla J., Sandra R. Hughes, and Berit M. Lakey. *Transforming Board Structure: Strategies for Committees and Task Forces.* Washington, DC: BoardSource,* 2001.

Carver, John. *Boards That Make a Difference: A New Design for Leadership in Nonprofit and Public Organizations.* San Francisco, CA: Jossey-Bass, 1997.

Chait, Richard P. *The Effective Board of Trustees.* Washington, DC: American Council on Education/Oryx Series on Higher Education, 1991.

Chait, Richard P. *How to Help Your Board Govern More and Manage Less.* Washington, DC: BoardSource,* 2003.

Ingram, Richard T. *Ten Basic Responsibilities of Nonprofit Boards.* Washington, DC: BoardSource,* 2003.

*Formerly the National Center for Nonprofit Boards

Light, Mark. *The Strategic Board: The Step-by-Step Guide to High-Impact Governance.* San Francisco, CA: Jossey-Bass, 2001.

National Association of Independent Schools. *Principles of Good Practice for Independent Schools.* Washington, DC.

O'Connell, Brian. *Board Overboard: Laughs and Lessons for All But the Perfect Nonprofit.* San Francisco, CA: Jossey-Bass, 1995.

Robinson, Maureen K. *Nonprofit Boards That Work: The End of One-Size-Fits-All Governance.* New York, NY: John Wiley & Sons, Inc., 2001.

Taylor, Barbara E., Richard P. Chait, and Thomas P. Holland. "The New Work of the Nonprofit Board." *Harvard Business Review,* September-October 1996.

• • • • • • • • • • • • • • • • • • •

CHAPTER 11

PERFORMING THE ROLE OF TRUSTEES

AS A TRUSTEE, you manage a multitude of roles, assignments, and relationships with good humor and good sense. At times you don't have sufficient hours in the day and your finances seem stretched to the limit, and yet you continue your commitment to the school. It must be a very special place!

Scattered throughout this handbook are many specific responsibilities and actions required of trustees as they exercise their governance role. How can you perform this distinctive role with integrity? It begins with understanding what it truly means to hold the school in trust and how you should conduct yourself in all of your roles and relationships.

Trustees have legal and financial responsibilities for the school, but as trust holders they have a much deeper attachment to the school — its mission, students, and faculty. Trustees have a profound understanding of the school's character and identity, champion it as it is now, and visualize what it can be in the future. Their connection to the school is deep and personal.

DUTIES OF CARE, LOYALTY, AND OBEDIENCE

Haven't I got enough duties as it is?

There are certain standards of conduct that trustees must meet as they fulfill their responsibilities. Often these are described as the duties of care, loyalty, and obedience.

THE DUTY OF CARE

The duty of care describes the level of competence expected of a trustee. State nonprofit corporate laws offer various definitions of this duty in suitable legalese, but they all come down to the importance of trustees' making good decisions with reasonable care. Trustees do not need to make perfect decisions; they do not need to be experts in child development and education. However, they need to recognize that they should hire people to provide the necessary wisdom, skill, and expertise to enact the school's program and mission. Trustees also need to set up policies and procedures to avoid risks to the school's financial well-being and to the health and safety of its students and staff.

THE DUTY OF LOYALTY

The duty of loyalty is the standard of faithfulness to the school. When making decisions, a trustee must put the school first. This duty is the basis for conflict of interest policies that are designed to prevent board members from enriching themselves, their families, and their friends at the expense of the school and from favoring one segment of the school over another. There will be more on conflicts of interest later in this chapter.

THE DUTY OF OBEDIENCE

The duty of obedience requires trustees to be true to the school's mission. Board members can exercise their own reasoned judgment in how the school can best achieve its mission. But they cannot act in a manner that is inconsistent with that mission. This duty is based on the principle that the school's constituents and the public at large must be able to act in confidence that what they are told about the school is true. If there is a discrepancy between the trustees' understanding of the school's mission and goals and that of the head, the results can be disastrous for all involved with the school. If the disconnection exists between the trustees and the school's constituents and the public at large, the result is the loss of institutional integrity — another form of disaster.

CONFLICTS OF INTEREST

Trustees tend to be active, involved, and influential people. Most are deeply connected to the school and are sought out for just those reasons. However, this means that they have some loyalties that may compete with each other and with the school and their colleagues. In Chapter 1, there was a brief description of the role of board members in identifying and managing any conflicts of interest they may have. The board and individual trustees can take steps to ensure that all trustees fulfill their obligation to separate personal interests from those of the school. For trustees, the school comes first.

> If I have all of these duties, how can I protect myself?

BOARDS CAN

- Adopt a conflict of interest policy that enjoins trustees or their family members from gaining financial or personal advantage from their board service. This policy should be drafted by legal counsel and adopted by the board. (See the Sample Materials section of this chapter for a sample policy.)
- Ask every trustee to sign an annual statement that acknowledges that they understand the conflicts of interest policy and to list any current or potential conflicts they have involving their board work.
- Orient new trustees to the conflict of interest policy and how it plays out in practice. Give examples of the types of conflicts typically found within independent school boards.
- Have periodic discussions at board meetings on why the conflict of interest policy protects the school and all trustees from being involved improperly in board decisions. These discussions can also help keep the school from being perceived as an institution whose trustees can better their personal and financial situations by their board service. This conversation can be especially appropriate when setting tuition with parent-trustees on the board.
- Establish a tradition that the board will deal openly on all matters that come before it.
- Hire an outside investment manager for the endowment funds; have a yearly financial audit by an independent auditor; and require an independent appraisal of any property given to the school.
- Establish a policy that all major contracts for goods and services will be put out to bid.

TRUSTEES CAN

- Sign the annual statement that they understand the conflict of interest policy and list all current and potential conflicts. If they are not sure what constitutes a conflict, they should consult the chair, who may put them in touch with the school's counsel.
- Be conscious of any conflicts that may arise after making the list and bring them to the attention of the chair.
- If a conflict does arise, make sure the board knows what the situation is and recuse themselves from the discussion and vote. Make sure that the minutes reflect this action.
- Always keep board discussions and decisions confidential, including those whose disclosure might benefit a relative, friend, or business associate.
- Whenever they are not sure if one of their biases is coloring their approach to a problem or decision, ask themselves, "What must the board do that is in the best interest of the school as a whole?" Not every trustee will agree on the specific answer to that question, but it will keep all board members focused on their trustee role as keeper of the mission for the total school.

Trustees' success at avoiding conflicts of interest depends upon the board's willingness to develop policies, follow them rigorously, and encourage open discussion on all issues. Such success also depends on the ability of individual trustees to govern themselves with integrity and hold the school in trust. Failing to do so can open the board and individual members up to lawsuits alleging that their self-interest has harmed the school, which unfortunately can be true. Above all, the abrogation of the duty of loyalty can create distrust and ruin the morale of the board, head, and staff — not to mention that of the students, parents, and graduates.

OTHER STANDARDS OF CONDUCT

What are some of the other standards of behavior that are evidenced by effective trustees who truly serve as guardians of the school? The following amplifies the subject matter of Chapter 1 and its focus on NAIS's Principles of Good Practice for Independent School Trustees.

GOOD PRINCIPLES FOR GOOD PRACTICE

Trustees are expected to support the school's mission and the resulting strategic plan and to give and get funds that help fulfill the mission and plan. How should they do this? They need to be visible in all of their various activities, since they are models for the school community. Their financial contributions should be among the earliest given, at the highest level their circumstances allow, and donated with good cheer. Their responses to questions about the school should be honest and as positive as possible, and their commitment to the strategic plan should be demonstrated through active participation in activities that further the plan. They should seek out formal and informal opportunities to spread the word about the wonderful school they serve. Trustees inspire others to believe in the school and to support it with their time, expertise, and funds.

You mean I need to speak out?

ACCEPTING RESPONSIBILITY FOR THE BOARD'S EFFECTIVENESS

Trustees exercise their major governance responsibilities through collective actions, which occur at board meetings. Showing up at meetings is the first step, but it is only the beginning. Trustees need to be aware that they are responsible for board decisions whether they are present or not. In fact, if trustees vote no on an issue, they are still liable if it goes forward, unless they get their names recorded in the minutes as voting against the motion or writing a letter to indicate their opposition. Although the board chair is charged with presiding at board meetings, board members need to accept responsibility for the meetings' effectiveness. They do this by:

The board is not a quarterly tea party!

- Keeping the school's mission as the basis of all major decisions. (Putting the mission statement on the wall of the room where board meetings are held can help trustees focus on the major priorities that stem from that mission.)
- Actively listening to others.
- Owning their opinions and stating them succinctly.
- Staying on point in their statements and encouraging others to do likewise.
- Asking clarifying questions.
- Knowing parliamentary procedure and using it when it can further the board's work. (For a short version of parliamentary procedure, see the Sample Materials in Chapter 10.)

- Helping the members of the board to reach a conclusion, knowing that not deciding is a decision.

Trustees should exhibit this same behavior beyond the board table at committee meetings and other school gatherings.

TRUE COMMITMENT

You mean I do need to show up?

Remember, when board members are chronically absent from meetings, the board loses its expertise and wisdom. This subverts the very reason members were elected to the board. Board chairs need to counsel such delinquent members, assuring them they are missed, learning if they feel disengaged and why, and asking them to consider ways other than board service to demonstrate their commitment to the school if they cannot attend meetings.

COMPLETE SUPPORT FOR BOARD DECISIONS

How can I support that decision? I didn't vote for it!

Once the board has made a decision, trustees must act within the duty of loyalty — which means they must support the decision once it becomes "public" even if they opposed it. This circumstance does not arise often, but when it does, trustees find it very stressful. However, if the board's deliberations leading to the proposal's adoption were informed and thoughtful, "losing" trustees may be comforted by the fact that every board member understood the question, had the school's best interests at heart, and still valued them as full members of the board. The majority just did not agree with the minority! If the matter is of such great importance that the opposing trustees cannot support the conclusion in public, they need to resign. Such resignations are very few, but boards should not rescind previous decisions to appease a few unhappy trustees who threaten resignation, especially if a strong majority believes the action was right.

CONFIDENTIALITY

What's so important about keeping it a secret?

Another trustee obligation is to keep all discussions and decisions confidential until, if ever, the board determines it is appropriate for the information to leave the boardroom. The issue of confidentiality runs throughout this handbook because it is so critical to the effective functioning of the board. Although "secrecy" sounds so negative in our open society, there are topics and circumstances that require it. The need for confidentiality may be a matter of timing, as when a board begins a preliminary examination of major changes in a school (adding to the faculty workload, acquiring a neighboring property, going coeducational, etc.). Or the subject matter itself may require strict confidence (when there is discontent with the head's performance, a negative self-assessment of the board's performance, allegations of a massive student drug problem, etc.).

TRUSTEE STANDARDS

Much of what has been stated in this handbook makes it appear as if trustees have to be perfect to serve their school effectively. If that were true, no one would be capable of governing and leading. The standards for trustee performance need to be high because boards want only the best for their school, including the best trustees. Remember that it is through the  collective expertise, wisdom, and actions of board members that good governance occurs. Individual trustees may find themselves in different places during their time of service, capable of giving more time or treasure at one point and less at another. Trustees are human, after all. However, there can be no compromise over the commitment to the school's mission; observation of the duties of care, loyalty, and obedience; and the basic integrity of all trustees.

FUNDAMENTAL QUESTIONS

As a trustee, you are responsible for your own actions and opinions. You dedicate yourself to working diligently and thoughtfully for the school through your governance role. You ask yourself three fundamental questions throughout your trusteeship:

- Do I add value to the work and life of the board and to the school?
- Am I learning from my experiences, both from my board work and my board-related educational opportunities, and am I improving my effectiveness?
- Am I having fun?

If the answer to all three questions is not yes, then trusteeship may not be for you. But if your responses are resoundingly positive, you may be just the sort of leader your school needs to advance the cause of children and education. Never forget that you are the guardian of the well-being of the school of today and tomorrow. You are a trust holder.

CASE STUDY

DETERMINING THE BOUNDS OF BOARD AUTHORITY

Over spring break, parents of two of School X's students filed a sexual harassment suit on behalf of their children against the board and against Tim Davis, a popular coach. The suit alleges that board members knowingly created a hostile climate for female students in two ways: (1) by retaining Davis after one allegation of harassment against him was filed (and ultimately dismissed in court), and (2) by failing to fully and properly investigate all such charges against faculty. Lawyers for the board contend that it is not the responsibility of board members to constitute an investigatory body for charges of harassment and those investigations should be left to the proper authorities.

What are the issues?
What should the board do?
What should the board chair do?
What should the head do?

S A M P L E   M A T E R I A L S

CONFLICT OF INTEREST STATEMENT FOR A BOARD OF TRUSTEES

Trustees are appointed/elected to serve [name of school] and its constituencies. The men and women who accept this position are expected to carry out their duties in a manner that inspires and assures the confidence of the school and the broader community.

The Trustees shall exercise the utmost good faith in all transactions touching upon their duties to the organization and its property. In their dealings with and on behalf of the organization, they are held to a strict rule of honest and fair dealing between themselves and the organization. They shall not use their positions as Trustees, or knowledge gained therefrom, so that a conflict might arise between the school's interest and that of any individual Trustee.

A conflict of interest arises in any situation in which a Trustee (and his or her immediate family) is involved in an activity that could adversely affect his or her judgment with respect to the business of the school or otherwise diminish the interest of the organization. When such a conflict arises, the individual with the conflict is expected to disclose in writing the existence of the conflict.

RESOURCES

Andringa, Robert C. *The Nonprofit Board Answer Book II: Beyond the Basics.* Washington, DC: BoardSource,* 2002.

Andringa, Robert C. and Ted W. Engstrom. *Nonprofit Board Answer Book: Practical Guidelines for Board Members and Chief Executives.* Washington, DC: BoardSource,* 2001.

Carver, John. *Boards That Make a Difference: A New Design for Leadership in Nonprofit and Public Organizations.* San Francisco, CA: Jossey-Bass, 1997.

Dambach, Charles, Oliver Tessier, and Carol Weisman. *The Business Professional's Guide to Nonprofit Board Service.* Washington, DC: BoardSource,* 2002.

Greenleaf, Robert, Don M. Frick, and Larry C. Spears (Eds.). *On Becoming a Servant Leader: The Private Writings of Robert K. Greenleaf.* San Francisco, CA: Jossey-Bass, 1996.

*Formerly the National Center for Nonprofit Boards

Kurtz, Daniel. *Managing Conflicts of Interest: Practical Guidelines for Nonprofit Boards.* Washington, DC: BoardSource,* 2001.

Leifer, Jacqueline C. and Michael B. Glomb. *Legal Obligations of Nonprofit Boards: A Guidebook for Board Members.* Washington, DC: BoardSource,* 1997.

Principles of Good Practice for Independent School Trustees. Washington, DC: National Association of Independent Schools, 2002. (Part of a complete set of Principles of Good Practice for Independent Schools.)

Widmer, Candace and Susan Houchin. *The Art of Trusteeship: The Nonprofit Board Member's Guide to Effective Governance.* San Francisco, CA: Jossey-Bass, 2000.

ADDITIONAL RESOURCES

The following is a list of organizations, publications, and websites that can be of help to independent school trustees. Many of the organizations provide services for members only. Some offer workshops that are open to nonmembers. Others provide consulting services for a fee.

ORGANIZATIONS

Alumni Program Council for Independent Schools

1825 Connecticut Ave., NW, Suite 670
Washington, DC 20009-5708
(202) 518-8633
www.apcnetwork.org
A well-established organization that plans an annual series of workshops across the country. Offers a newsletter and other resources for alumni programs.

Association of Governing Boards of Universities and Colleges

One Dupont Circle, Suite 400
Washington, DC 20036
(202) 296-8400
www.agb.org
Dedicated to strengthening the performance of boards of public and private higher education. Offers workshops and publications that may also be useful to independent schools.

BoardSource
(formerly the National Center for Nonprofit Boards)

1828 L St., NW, Suite 900
Washington, DC 20036-5114
(202) 452-6262 or (800) 883-6262
www.boardsource.org
Plans an annual conference each fall and offers a number of monographs designed to help boards improve. Serves a broad range of nonprofit organizations.

Council for Advancement and Support of Education

1307 New York Ave., NW, Suite 1000
Washington, DC 20005-4701
(202) 328-5900
www.case.org
Supports a wide range of programs about fund raising, alumni relations, and communications for four-year and two-year colleges and independent schools. Each winter, the association co-hosts the CASE/NAIS Independent Schools Conference.

Educational Directions, Inc.

156 Anthony Rd.
Portsmouth, RI 02871-0768
(401) 683-3523
www.edu-directions.com/
A consulting and publishing firm that offers newsletters by subscription, including the *Trustee's Letter* and the *Head's Letter.*

Harvard Business School Executive Education

Soldiers Field
Boston, MA 02163-9986
(800) HBS-5577, ext. 7011
www.exed.hbs.edu
Often in conjunction with the Graduate School of Education, the Executive Education division offers a variety of programs and workshops, all with useful leadership and management resources. Harvard Business School Publishing (*http://harvardbusinessonline.hbsp.harvard.edu*) offers *Harvard Business Review,* books, newsletters, and more.

Independent School Chairpersons Association

17 E. 84th St., #4A
New York, NY 10028
(212) 570-6605
www.iscachairs.org
A membership organization for board chairs at independent schools. Holds several annual programs and offers a member listserve.

Independent School Management

1316 N. Union St.
Wilmington, DE 19806-2594
(302) 656-4944
www.isminc.com
A research, analysis, and consulting firm devoted to the management needs of independent schools. ISM produces two advisory publications, *Ideas & Perspectives* and *To the Point,* and offers administrative workshops.

National Association of College and University Business Officers

2501 M St., NW, Suite 400
Washington, DC 20037
(202) 861-2500
www.nacubo.org
A professional organization whose members are chief administrative and financial officers at more than 2,100 colleges and universities. But its programs and publications may be of use to schools.

National Association of Corporate Directors

1828 L St., NW, Suite 801
Washington, DC 20036
(202) 775-0509
www.nacdonline.org
The only membership organization devoted to improving the performance of corporate boards. In addition to publishing a newsletter, *Director's Monthly,* NACD conducts educational programs and standard-setting research on board governance issues and practices. Most members are for-profit corporations.

National Association of Independent Schools

1620 L St., NW, Suite 1100
Washington, DC 20036-5695
(202) 973-9700
www.nais.org

A membership organization for more than 1,200 member schools and associations in the United States and abroad, NAIS is the national institutional advocate for independent precollegiate education.

GENERAL NEWSLETTERS AND MAGAZINES

- *Board Member,* a magazine published 10 times a year by BoardSource (formerly the National Center for Nonprofit Boards). Available to members only. (202) 452-6262 or *www.boardsource.org.*

- *Director's Monthly,* a newsletter about governance published monthly by the National Association of Corporate Directors. Available to members only. (202) 775-0509 or *www.nacdonline.org/publications.*

- *E-volunteerism: The Electronic Journal of the Volunteer Community.* Quarterly online newsletter available by subscription. (215) 438-8342 or *www.e-volunteerism.com/subscribe.html.*

- *Head's Letter,* a newsletter published nine times a year by Educational Directions, Inc. (401) 683-3523 or *www.edu-directions.com/.*

- *Ideas & Perspectives,* a newsletter published 16 times a year by Independent School Management. (302) 656-4944 or *www.isminc.com.*

- *Independent School,* a quarterly magazine published by NAIS. Available by subscription to members and nonmembers: (800) 793-6701 or *www.nais.org/pubs/pubs_list.cfm.*

- *Trustee's Letter,* a newsletter published five times a year by Educational Directions, Inc. (401) 683-3523 or *www.edu-directions.com/.*

KEY WEBSITES

Alumni Program Council for Independent Schools:
www.apcnetwork.org

Association of Governing Boards of Universities and Colleges:
www.agb.org

Harvard Business School Executive Education:
www.exed.hbs.edu

Independent School Association of the Central States:
www.isacs.org

National Association of Independent Schools:
www.nais.org
(*Note:* The NAIS website is hyperlinked to member local, state, and
regional association sites.)

PARLIAMENTARY GLOSSARY

Accept — Same as adopt, approve, or carry. Motions are accepted, approved, adopted, or carried. Reports, with the exception of the external audit report, are not accepted, approved, adopted, or carried.

Ad hoc — A Latin term meaning "for this case alone" and used to designate a special or short-term committee. (Pronounced *add HOCK.*)

Adopt — Same as accept, approve, or carry.

Agenda — An outline of the order of business for the chair and board to use during a meeting.

Amend — Modify, change, or improve a motion before it is adopted or rejected.

Announcing the vote — Declaration by the chair of the result of the vote.

Approve — Same as accept, adopt, or carry.

Are you ready for the question? — Debate discussion is now in order.

Authority (parliamentary) — The authority adopted by an assembly to govern parliamentary procedure during its meetings, usually *Robert's Rules of Order, Newly Revised.*

Aye and no — Terms used in voice voting. (*Aye* is pronounced *I*.)

Budget — An itemized estimate of income and expenses.

Bylaws — A document, adopted by the board or a society, which contains the basic rules for governing that board or organization.

Call for the orders of the day — A motion used to call for a return to the scheduled order of business.

Carry — Same as accept, approve, or adopt.

Chair — The presiding officer. Authority is vested in the office, not in the person.

Commit — To place a proposition in the hands of a committee.

Consent agenda — Part of a meeting agenda in which items of routine business are approved as a group by unanimous consent. Financial reports should never be included in this section of the agenda.

Division of the assembly — The motion calls for a rising vote.

Division of the question — Separating a motion in two or more distinct parts for the purpose of debating and voting upon each part separately.

Ex officio — By virtue of office. The bylaws often provide that the chair is an ex-officio member of all committees. This means the head must be notified of all meetings, has voice and vote, but is not included in the quorum. To deny an ex-officio member a vote, the bylaws should state that the individual serves "ex officio without a vote." (Pronounced *EX eh-FISH-ee-o*.)

General consent — Informal agreement of the assembly. A form of voting in which there is no dissenting vote, as in "If there is no objection...."

Germane — Closely related; of the same subject matter. Example: An amendment must be germane to the motion to which it is applied.

Illegal vote — A vote that cannot be credited to any candidate or choice but is counted in determining the number of votes cast for the purpose of computing the majority.

Immediate pending question — The last question stated by the chair when several questions are pending, sometimes called the "last pending question."

Incidental motions — Those that arise out of a pending question rather than from the business itself. Example: Request for information, suspension of the rules, etc.

Main motion — One that introduces a subject to the assembly for discussion and action.

Majority vote — More than half of the votes cast by persons legally entitled to vote.

Pending question — One that is before the board or assembly. A question is pending from the time it is stated by the chair until it is disposed of, either temporarily or permanently.

Plurality vote — The largest portion of the votes cast when there are more than two choices. A plurality vote never decides a question or constitutes an election except by specific rule of the board or organization.

Precedence — Priority in order or rank in which motions are considered and acted on.

Precedent — An established custom or preceding instance or case that, in absence of a rule, may serve as an example or justification in future similar cases.

Previous question — Motion to close debate and take the vote at once on the immediately pending question. The first vote is to close debate; if that vote passes, the board immediately (without any further debate) votes on the pending question. If the vote does not carry, debate on the pending question continues.

Pro tem — Temporarily; usually applies to one who serves in the absence of a regular officer or chair of a committee. (From the Latin *pro tempore;* pronounced *pro TEM.*)

Quorum — The number of members required to be present so that the assembly may transact business. The quorum is a majority of all members, unless the bylaws state otherwise.

Ratify — An incidental main motion to approve action already taken. Requires a vote of the board or assembly to make the action valid.

Reconsider — The motion to bring up a motion already adopted, which must be made by a member of the board who voted with the prevailing side. This motion is in order only during the meeting at which the original motion was made.

Rescind — To strike out an entire main motion, resolution, rule, bylaw, section, or paragraph that has been adopted at some previous time; or to amend something previously adopted and change only a part of the text; or to substitute a different version. These motions are in order, provided that none of the action involved has been carried out in a way that is too late to undo and provided that the question cannot be decided by calling up a motion to reconsider. A negative vote on these motions can be reconsidered, but not an affirmative vote.

Revision of bylaws — A complete set of bylaws submitted as a substitute for existing bylaws.

Seriatum — Considered by paragraph. (Pronounced *sear-ee-AH-tem.*)

Sine die — Latin for "without a day." Adjournment without a time set for the next meeting. (Pronounced *SEE-nay DEE-ee.*)

Standing rules — Rules of a temporary or semi-permanent nature, relating to administrative details or organizational procedures. Standing rules remain in force until amended or rescinded.

Tie vote — Less than a majority. (A motion is lost when there is a tie vote. The chair may vote to break a tie, but if the matter is of major importance, the chair needs to be very sure that the matter is the right thing for the board to do at that time.)

Two-thirds vote — Two out of three votes cast. Example: For two-thirds approval, the affirmative vote is at least twice as large as the negative.

Unanimous (general) consent — Used when there is no opposition in the course of routine business or on questions of little importance. Often used to pass minutes, close a meeting, or adopt a consent agenda. To obtain unanimous consent, the chair states, *"If there is no objection..."* (or *"Without objection..."*) the action the chair mentions will be taken. Alternatively, the chair may ask, *"Is there any objection to...?"* The chair then pauses. If no member calls out, *"I object,"* the chair announces, *"Since there is no objection ..."* the action is decided upon. If anyone does object, the regular deliberative process must take place.

Unfinished business — Matters on the agenda of a previous meeting on which no action was taken.

Viva voce — Voice vote, as when the chair says, "All those in favor, say aye; all those opposed, say no." (Pronounced *VEE-va VO-see.*)

Withdraw a motion — To remove a motion from consideration by the board or assembly upon request by the mover, and by permission of the board or assembly if the motion has been stated by the chair.

INDEX

Accountability, 63
Accreditation, 72
Action plans, 66–67, 74, 76
Administrators, 160–162. *See also* Head of school
Admissions, 49–50, 183
Advancement committee, 175
Advisory councils, 110
Agendas (sample), 187
Alumni, 108, 164–165
Alumni Program Council for Independent Schools, 203
American Red Cross, 44
Angell, Roger, 93
Annual operational plans, 74
Anti-discrimination laws, 33
Association of Governing Boards of Universities and Colleges, 203
Audit committee, 175
Audit Committee Due Diligence Checklist (sample), 42–44

Barbieri, Richard, 39, 114, 143, 156
Baseball, 93, 152–153
Bassett, Patrick F., xi, 30, 190
Berra, Yogi, 152, 153
Board development. *See* Recruitment of trustees
Board of directors, ix
Board profile grid, 117–119
Boarding schools, 96, 176
BoardSource, 204
Budgets, 70, 74. *See also* Fiscal responsibilities
Buildings and grounds, 35, 174–175
Burgin, Walter, 61
Bylaws, 7, 31

executive committee, 176
nomination of trustees, 102
recruitment of trustees, 95–96
renomination of trustees, 100–101
responsibilities of officers, 181

Capital campaigns, 62
Capital giving, 12. *See also* Fund raising
Care, Duty of, 194
Case studies
administrative evaluations, 156
bounds of board authority, 200
changes in school constituents, 169
classroom problems, 143
diversity, 87, 113
financial aid to students, 114
hiring the head of school, 142
policies, 55
relations between the head of school and board chair, 155
self-evaluation of boards, 186
strategic planning, 75
trustee responsibilities, 38–39
Chairs (presidents) of boards, 101–102, 145–157
communicating bad news, 154
communications with head of school, 150–151. *See also* Head of school
compared to head of school, 148
disciplining of trustees, 151
impact of turnover, 148–149
joint responsibilities with head of school, 147–148. *See also* Head of school
relations with trustees, 160
responsibilities of, 145–148, 181–182
running of meetings, 177–178

supporting head of school, 153
teamwork metaphors for
    relationship to head of school,
    151–153
Chait, Richard P., 51, 112
Closed meetings, 180–181
Commitment letter, trustee and school
    (sample), 122–123
Committee on trustees, 93–105
    bylaws and, 95–96
    cultivating candidates, 98–100
    developing candidate criteria, 97–98
    exit interviews, 105
    job description (sample), 116
    of officers for the board, 101–102
    orientations for new trustees, 103
    recognition of trustees, 104–105
    renomination of trustees, 100–101
    time commitment of, 94–95
Committees, 2–3, 17, 173–176
    admissions/marketing, 183
    audit, 175
    development/advancement, 175
    education, 183–184
    executive, 175–176
    finance, 174–175
    financial aid, 184
    head's advisory, 183
    personnel, 184
    for recruitment of trustees, 93–105. See
        also Committee on trustees
    strategic planning, 184. See also
        Strategic planning
    student life, 184
Communications, 139
    of action plans, 67, 68
    of bad news, 154
    between board chair and head of
        school, 150–151
    at meetings, 178
    of policies, 52–53
Compensation to heads of schools, 33–34,
    129, 130, 134
Confidentiality, 19, 136, 198–199
Conflicts of interest, 19, 195–196, 201
Constituent relations, 9, 159–170
    administrators and faculty, 160–162
    alumni, 164–165
    current students, 165–166
    donors, 109, 167
    educational associations, 168
    friends of school, 167
    neighbors, 168
    parents, 162–164
Consultants, 63–64

Contracts, 195
    for head of school, 128, 131–132, 134
    third-party, 31, 32
Corporate laws, 31
Corporations, 109, 171–172
Council for Advancement and Support of
    Education, 204
Creeds of schools, 28. See also Mission
    statements
Crisis planning, 49
Curriculum development, 50

Day-to-day management, 11
Decisions, 19, 136, 198
Demographics, 97. See also Diversity on
    boards
Development committee, 35–36, 175
Discrimination, 33, 87, 113
Diversity in student body, 70–71
Diversity on boards, 15, 97, 106–109
Donors. See Fund raising
Drucker, Peter, xi, 159
Dupree, Max, 61
Duties of trustees, 194. See also Standards
    of conduct for trustees

Education committee, 183–184
Educational associations, 168, 203–207
Educational Directions, Inc., 204
The Effective Board of Trustees (Chait), 112
Employment Retirement Income Security
    Act (ERISA), 33
Employment terms, 50
Enrollment, 70
Evaluations
    case study on, 156
    of head of school, 13–14, 129–131
    of strategic plan, 68
    of trustees, 96–97
Executive committee, 175–176
Executive session, 134
Exit interviews, 105
Expenditures, 70. See also Fiscal
    responsibilities

Faculty, 50, 70
    relations with board, 160–162
    as trustees, 108
Fair Labor Standards Act, 33
Fiduciary responsibilities, 27–45. See also
    Standards of conduct for trustees
    financial, 34–36
    legal, 30–34
    mission statements, 28–39
    risk management, 36–37

Financial aid committee, 184
Financial aid to students, 21, 70, 114
Fiscal responsibilities, 11–13, 34–36
    budgeting for legal counsel, 53
    budgets, 70, 74
    finance committee, 174–175
    Interim Statement of Activity (sample),
        41
    policies set for, 49
    strategic planning for, 69–70
    trustee giving, 99, 120
Foundations, 109
Frequency of meetings, 180
Fund raising, 11, 12
    development committee, 35–36, 175
    giving trends, 71
    recruitment of trustees, 98
    relations with funders, 167
    trustee giving, 99, 120

Gates, Bill, 79
Goals, 73, 130
Governance committee. *See* Committee
    on trustees
Governance through Partnership
    program, 104, 144
Graduates of schools, 108, 164–165
Graham, Katharine, 193

Harvard Business School Executive
    Education, 204
Head of school, 13–15, 127–144
    advisory to, 183
    average tenure for, 149
    communications with board chair,
        150–151
    compared to chair of board, 148
    compensation to, 129, 130, 134
    contracts for, 128, 131–132, 134
    evaluation of, 129–131
    executive session, 134
    hiring of, 128
    implementation of policies, 51–52
    informal times with, 140–141
    joint responsibilities with chair of
        board, 147–148
    relationship with board, 56, 135–139
    responsibilities of, 128
    setting policies, 49–50
    teamwork metaphors for relationship
        to board chair, 151–153
    termination of employment, 132–134
Hiring head of school, 128
HIV/AIDS policies, 51
Holland, Thomas P., 51

Honorary trustees, 110
Houle, Cyril, 148

Independent School Chairpersons
    Association, 205
Independent School Management, 205
Independent schools, definition of, x
Information gathering, 64–65
Institute for New Heads, 144
Institutional policies, 11. *See also* Policies
Interim Statement of Activity (sample), 41
Interviews, 65, 105
Investments, 35, 174

Jordan, Barbara, 47

Lawrence-Lightfoot, Sara, 5
Laws (local, state, and federal), 32–34. *See
    also* Legal requirements
Lawsuits, 36–37. *See also* Risk
    management
Leadership through Partnership program,
    144, 150
Legal requirements, 7–8
    open or closed meetings, 180–181
    responsibilities of trustees, 30–34
    separate legal counsel, 53
Loyalty, Duty of, 194

Magazines, 206
Management, day-to-day, 11
Manuals for boards, 115
Marketing committee, 183
Massey, William F., 69
Meetings of board, 21–22, 177–181, 187
Mentors, 102
Minutes of meetings, 17, 178, 179, 182
Mission statements, 6–7, 10, 73
    policies working with, 53, 61
    responsibility of board members to
        uphold, 28–30, 194
Monetary gifts, 12. *See also* Fund raising
Multiculturalism, 107–108. *See also*
    Diversity on boards
Multiple-year contracts, 132

National Association of College and
    University Business Officers, 205
National Association of Corporate
    Directors, 205
National Association of Independent
    Schools (NAIS), 71, 206
    assessment instruments for trustees,
        96, 104
    compensation statistics, 129

contracts for heads of schools, 128
data from, 65
number of trustees on a board, 177
open meetings, 181
Principles of Good Practice, 6–20,
    23–25, 106, 124. *See also* Principles
    of Good Practice
strategic planning model, 68
tuition statistics, 21
National Center for Nonprofit Boards, 204
Neighbors to schools, 168
Newsletters, 206
Nominating committee. *See* Committee
    on trustees

Obedience, Duty of, 194
Objectives, 73–74
Officers on the board, 101–102, 121,
    181–183
Open meetings, 180–181
Operational policies, 11
Organization of board, 17, 171–191
    committees, 173–176
    meetings, 177–181, 187
    nonprofit and for-profit comparison,
        171–172
    officers, 101–102, 121, 181–183. *See
        also* Chair of board
    size of board, 177
    structures, 173
Orientations, 16, 103

Parent/teacher associations, 163
Parents
    disagreements with heads of
        schools, 138
    relations with board, 162–164
    as trustees, ix, 18, 108, 109
Parliamentary procedure, 179, 188–189,
    209
Personnel committee, 184
Philosophies of schools, 28, 73. *See also*
    Mission statements
Physical assets, 35
Planning. *See* Strategic planning
Policies, 31–32, 47–59
    checklist for forming, 57–58
    communicating, 52–53
    on conflicts of interest, 195
    development of, 49–50
    operational, 11
    procedures for forming, 51–52
    reasons for, 48
    and strategic planning, 61
Powell, Arthur G., 27

Principles of good practice, 5–25, 196–197
    for boards, 23
    equity and justice, 124
    fiscal responsibilities, 11–13
    individual responsibilities, 18–20, 24
    legal requirements, 7–8
    mission statements, 6–7
    organization of board, 17
    recruitment and retention of
        members, 15–16
    relationship with head of school,
        135–139
    strategic planning, 8–9
Professional development, 16, 103–104
Profile grid for board members, 117–119
Property of schools, 35, 174–175
Public relations, 63
Publications, 37, 68, 206

Recognition of trustees, 104–105
Records of meetings, 17
Recruitment of trustees, 15, 93–125
    advisory councils, 110
    board manual contents, 115
    board profile grid, 117–119
    bylaws, 95–96
    committee for, 93–105. *See also*
        Committee on trustees
    dimensions of an effective board, 112
    diversity, 106–109
    former trustees, 110
    honorary trustees, 110
    job description (sample), 116
    officer qualifications, 121
    time and financial requirements, 120
    trustee/school commitment letter
        (sample), 122–123
Relations with constituents. *See*
    Constituent relations
Relations with head of school, 13–15,
    127–154. *See also* Head of school
Renomination of trustees, 100–101
Reports, 178, 180
Resignation from boards, 14
Resolution of differences, 138
Resources, 25, 45, 59, 77, 91, 125, 144,
    157, 170, 191, 202, 203–207
Retention of trustees, 104
Retreats for strategic planning, 66
Revenues, 69. *See also* Fiscal
    responsibilities
Risk management, 8, 36–37, 40
Robert's Rules of Order, Newly Revised, 7
Rogers, Will, 68

Safety issues, 50

Salaries, 33–34, 129, 130, 134

Secretary of board, 182

Size of board, 177

Sports metaphors, 151–153

Standards of conduct for trustees, 193–202. *See also* Fiduciary responsibilities

    accepting responsibility for board effectiveness, 197–198

    confidentiality, 198–199

    conflicts of interest, 195–196

    duties, 194

    principles of good practice, 196–197

    supporting decisions, 198

Strategic Indicators for Higher Education (Taylor and Massey), 69

Strategic planning, x, 61–77

    approval of, 67–68

    committee, 184

    cycles for, 71–73

    definitions of terms, 73–74

    development of, 65–67

    evaluation, 68

    indicators for independent schools, 68–71

    mission statements consistent with, 6–7

    people involved with, 63–64

    primary work of trustees, 8–9

    process of, 64–68

    reasons for, 62–63

Strategies, 74

Student/faculty ratios, 70

Student life committee, 184

Students, 165–166

    diversity among, 70–71

Students as trustees, 109

Sunshine Laws, 181

Surveys, 65

Task forces, 1–3

    assignments, 176, 181, 182

    buildings and grounds, 174

    diversity, 106

    for evaluations, 14

    executive committee, 176

    frequency of meetings, 180

    to increase board effectiveness, 17, 155, 173, 185

    for planning, 63–65, 184

    for recruitment of trustees, 98

Taylor, Barbara E., 51, 69, 173

Teachers, 50. *See also* Faculty

Teamwork metaphors, 151–153

Tennis, 152

Termination of employment for heads of schools, 132–134

Third-party contracts, 31, 32

Time commitment, 120

    committee on trustees, 94–95

    meetings, 179, 180, 198

Time management, 3

Topics for discussion (sample), 21–22

Training, 16, 103–104

Treasurer, 183

Trustee Handbook/Board Policies Book, 190

Trustees

    compared to board of directors, ix

    disciplining of, 151

    guidelines for new, 20

    list of necessary items for, 190

    standards of conduct for, 193–202

Tuition, 21

Turnover in leadership, 148–149

Vice chair of board, 182

Vision statements, 73

Websites, 207

Wheatley, Margaret J., 127, 171

Yearly operational plans, 74

Zoning issues, 168

ABOUT THE AUTHOR

Mary Hundley DeKuyper combines her vocation of consulting with nonprofits, especially on governance concerns, with her avocation of serving on boards. Many of the clients with whom she consults are independent schools, private and public institutions of higher education, and educational associations. DeKuyper is associated with BoardSource (formerly called the National Center for Nonprofit Boards) and the Association of Governing Boards of Universities and Colleges.

As a volunteer, DeKuyper has chaired 12 nonprofit boards and served on an additional 15. Currently, she is a trustee of Far Hills Country Day School in New Jersey. She is a former trustee of her alma mater, The Bryn Mawr School in Maryland, where she was president of the board (1984-1988) and of the alumnae association (1980-1982). She was a member and chair of the Association of Independent Maryland Schools' trustee committee. She serves as the national chair of volunteers of the American Red Cross, a full-time position at the highest level of the organization.